SHAKESPEARE'S
BOY ACTORS

Edward Kynaston, the last of the Boy Actors

GABRIELLE ENTHOVEN COLLECTION, VICTORIA AND
ALBERT MUSEUM

SHAKESPEARE'S
BOY ACTORS

W. ROBERTSON DAVIES
B.LITT. (OXON.)

*Illustrated
with eight
plates*

LONDON: J. M. DENT & SONS LTD

CONTENTS

ILLUSTRATIONS

CHAPTER I

The Position of the Boy Actors in the Elizabethan Theatre—
The Puritan Attack on the Theatre as it affected the Boys—The
Coming of Actresses after the Restoration — Contemporary
Evidence of the Ability of Boy Actors—Elizabethan Acting—
The Training of the Boys—Illusion in the Elizabethan Theatre

THE curious inquirer into the history of our theatre is
often amazed, as he picks his way through the wilder-
nesses of contemporary criticism, by the eulogies
which have been written on Mrs Siddons's performance as Lady Macbeth or about George Anne Bellamy
as Juliet, or Dora Jordan as Helena and Ophelia.   As
he reads of Fanny Kemble's Isabella or Helen Faucit's
Rosalind he is able to recapture something of the
enthusiasm which filled those earlier playgoers, and if
he is one of those happy creatures whose antiquarian
leanings enable him to exalt the past at the expense of
the present he may spend many pleasant hours recon-
structing those much admired performances.   In his
researches he will find that the dominating characteristic of them all is their superabundant femininity;
the womanly qualities of the actresses are extolled, and
their adherence to contemporary ideals of feminine
nature and their imposition of these upon the parts
they played is hailed as great acting in proportion to
its completeness.   The autobiographies of the actresses
themselves are filled with raptures about their Shakespearian roles, and during the nineteenth century the

B   I

transports become almost comic, so intensely do the ladies identify themselves with their favourites among Shakespeare's heroines. It was during this period that Helen Faucit wrote feelingly and self-revealingly of her experiences as an actress in Shakespeare, some of her roles evoking experiences almost mystical in character, and Mary Cowden-Clarke was so possessed by the reality of Shakespeare's women that she wrote *The Girlhood of Shakespeare's Heroines*, a very popular work, in which each one is equipped with the background of an entertaining childhood and such sweet traits as the ruder-minded Shakespeare had neglected to include in the plays. As he reads the player's memoirs the inquirer who does not become completely lost in them must often wonder if the madness which is commonly thought to afflict Shakespeare's critics does not also extend itself to his interpreters. Actresses both now and in the past have always been ready to defend their performances against criticism by eager and ingenious explanations of what Juliet or Lady Macbeth would do at certain moments of the play, knowledge which they acquire by processes not easily distinguishable from divination, and the general attitude of the theatrical world, the playgoer, and the reader toward Shakespeare's women is one of anthropomorphism. Even eminent critics, with undoubted sincerity, have written treatises on the psychology of the Shakespearian heroines, and have attempted to deduce from their actions and words Shakespeare's own concept of womanhood, producing monsters of wit and virtue modestly labelled Shakespeare's Ideal Woman.

In spite of this determined attempt to consider the
Shakespearian heroines as women it is doubtful if any
valid opinion can be reached upon them unless the fact
is kept in mind that all these roles were written to be
acted by boys, and that no English women are known
to have performed in the public theatre of his time.
Shakespeare's women, whatever characteristics may be
attributed to them in the void, were conceived to suit
the peculiar talents and limitations of the boy actor, for
it is only reasonable to suppose that the convention
whereby women, on the Elizabethan stage, were always
represented by male actors had an influence on the
technique of the dramatic authors of the time.   There
are certain detectable differences between the women's
roles in their plays and those written after the coming
of actresses to the stage.   The purpose of this brief
study is to find out what these differences are by making
a careful examination of the technique used in con-
structing the women's parts in Shakespeare's plays, and
to attempt some determination of the extent to which
Elizabethan drama was restricted or set free by the
convention of the boy actor.

The tradition of boy actors in England extends from
the beginnings of drama in the Middle Ages, when
church liturgy fathered the mystery and morality plays,
and the choir-boys assisted the clerks in their presentation.   Their own particular ceremony of the Boy
Bishop, which was performed on the eve of Holy
Innocents, has a strong dramatic flavour.   The lay
minstrels also, travelling in groups of four or more,
generally had one boy apprentice at least who played

the women's parts in the interludes which these performed, and likewise danced, tumbled, and sang, and probably acted as a servant to the rest of the troupe. These boys who led the rough life of wandering minstrels were the direct prototypes of the Elizabethan boy actors.

The Elizabethan players were ostensibly the servants of a nobleman whose livery they wore and whose name was their guarantee and protection; the boys were the servants of the actors. The stage was a profession to which a child might be put without reproach, and individual actors undertook to train boys whose services they sold to the company for a wage. Philip Henslowe's diary has an entry which reads:

bowght my boye Jeames brystow of william agusten player the 18 of Desemb₃ 1597 for viijˡˡ.

(F. 232, l. 26.)

and there is a later entry concerning the same boy as follows:

the companye dothe owe vnto me for my boye Jemes bristos wages from the 23 of Aprᵉll 1600 vnto the xv of febreary 1600 next after the ratte of iijˢ a weeke some vjˡˡ ixˢ.

(F. 85ᵛ, l. 31.)

From these two entries it may be deduced that Henslowe regarded the boy James Brystow as a personal investment, and he allowed him to serve the company for a wage which was payable to himself, and not to the boy. It is interesting to compare Brystow's wage with that of the child in Chapman's *May Day*, of whom is said by Quintiliano:

Afore heaven, 'tis a sweet faced child, me thinks he should

shew well in woman's attire. . . . I 'll help thee to three
crowns a week for him, and she can act well.

(Act III, Sc. III.)

The difference between three shillings and three crowns
is twelve shillings: it is possible that Bryſtow was a
beginner or an inferior actor, while the wage mentioned
in Chapman is that of a firſt-class boy, able to command
a high price. It is conceivable, also, that the fact
that he was renting Bryſtow to his own company
dulled the keen edge even of Henslowe's remarkable
rapacity.

The boys lived with their maſters as other apprentices did, and their treatment would depend very much
upon the circumſtances in which they found themselves. In some cases the relationship may have been
a very pleasant one; there is evidence in the Henslowe
diary that the boys carried messages and did minor
business duties for their maſters. Bryſtow witnessed
at leaſt one document for Henslowe. Edward Alleyn,
the famous actor of *Tamburlaine* and Henslowe's son-
in-law, had a boy with the arreſting name of John Pig,
who accompanied the mighty Ned on tour. There is
a letter yet extant written by Alleyn to his wife, couched
in intimate and humorous terms and signed 'John
Pyk,' which gives some hint of the amiable eſtimation
in which Pig was held by the Alleyns. It is a pity that
so little is known of Pig; surely with such a name his
career muſt have been intereſting.

The exact circumſtances under which the boys
entered the service of the elder actors are not clearly
determined. T. W. Baldwin, in his remarkable work

of research, *The Organization and Personnel of the Shake-spearian Company* (1927), assumes that they were apprenticed for a period of seven years, beginning at the age of ten years and becoming a full member of the company when they had served their time. There are practical objections to this theory; a boy of ten years old would be of very little use in the theatre except as a servant, and to play the parts of children or pages, for his lack of experience would prevent him from taking a woman's role. It is unlikely, also, that an actor would keep a boy and train him and lodge him unless it were possible to let him out to the company for some small wage. There is no evidence that the boy actors were subject to ordinary apprentice laws; there was no guild of actors, for they were, in law, members of a nobleman's retinue and the apprentice laws were meant primarily to be a convenience to the guilds. It is true, however, that certain actors were members of a guild of musicians and that their boys were doubtless bound to them by the conditions of that guild, but these formed a special class, and were not sufficiently numerous to be looked upon as typical. Sir Edmund Chambers, in his *William Shakespeare* (1930), is of the opinion that the boys were bound to their masters by private agreement only, and were not apprentices in law; he estimates the term of their service at two or three years. This latter theory fits the practical considerations of the theatre much better than Baldwin's, for it makes the term of service extensible, and allows for the natural variation by which some boys would retain their value as female

impersonators longer than others. It seems reasonable to suppose that the boys were bound to their
masters by private agreement at an age when they were
tall enough and intelligent enough to profit by training. Ten years of age seems very young for this; it
would be an exceptional boy who was ready for
training before he was twelve or thirteen.

The children's companies were conducted on rather
different lines, and in these the children were accepted
at the age of ten, or perhaps earlier. Ben Jonson says
of Salathiel Pavy, who was a child of Queen Elizabeth's
Chapel:

> Years he number'd scarce thirteen
>   When Fates turned cruel
> Yet three fill'd zodiacs had he been
>   The stage's jewel;
>
> (*Epigrammes*, cxx.)

Certainly a year of preliminary training would be
necessary before the boy appeared in any important
part. The actors in the children's companies, however, do not seem to have entered the adult companies
until they were themselves adults, preferring to take
advantage of the education which was given them at
the expense of the Crown. Nat Field, the actor-
dramatist, appears to have followed this course and to
have entered an adult company in 1600, to play a
leading part in Jonson's *Cynthia's Revels*.

Whatever the length of time during which they were
bound either to actors or sharers in the companies,
many of the boys seem to have remained in employ-
ment in some capacity until they were able to play
adult male roles. Gosson, in his polemic, *Playes*

confuted in Fiue Actions (1582), gives clear evidence of this when he writes:

> Most of the Players haue bene eyther men of occupations which they haue forsaken to lyue by playing, or common minstrels, or trayned vp from theire childhood to this abhominable exercise & haue now no other way to get theire liuinge. . . .
>
> (p. 215.)

The boys, when their obligation to their masters was fulfilled, may have been paid directly by the company, or they may have received some share of the wage which was paid to the master. Unhappily there is no evidence on this point which is a sufficient warrant for a definite statement, and the point is not of great importance. The fact that the usual term of apprenticeship in other trades was seven years would give the sanction of custom to the boy's attachment to his master even when his initial obligation was over. At any rate it is clear that the boys usually remained in the company until they were able to serve as full-fledged actors of men's parts.

The evidence concerning the position and talents of the boy actors is not extensive, but there is sufficient to provide a fairly complete picture of them. The continuous warfare between the players and the Puritans which raged from the time when the actors were mere itinerant bands until the theatres were closed in 1642 provoked a great deal of acrimonious pamphleteering on both sides, and there are frequent references to the boy actors. The players were immensely proud of their accomplishment, and re-

garded it as a sign of grace in themselves that they
employed no women, as was done on the Con-
tinent, and Thomas Nashe's defence, contained in
Pierce Penilesse his Supplication to the Diuell (1592), is
justly famous:

> . . . Our Players are not as the players beyond sea, a sort
> of squirting baudie Comedians, that haue whores and
> common Curtizans to playe women's parts, and forbeare no
> immodest speech or vnchast action that may procure
> laughter, but our Sceane is more stately furnisht than euer
> it was in the time of *Roscius*, our representations honorable,
> and full of gallant resolution, not consisting like theirs of
> a Pantaloun, a Whore, and a Zanie, but of Emperours,
> Kings and Princes: whose true Tragedies (*Sophocleo cothurno*)
> they doo vaunt.
>
> (p. 27.)

Classical precedent, also, forbade the appearance of
women on the stage, and Aristotle's classification of
women as inferior beings for the purpose of drama
doubtless carried weight with those playwrights who
sought salvation in the classic form. Women had
never appeared upon any stage which the English
actors considered worthy of imitation, and to them
there seemed no reason why women should act at all,
except in masques and those entertainments which
were arranged for private display.

The Puritans would have been equally scandalized by
the suggestion that women should appear on the stage,
but they had a bolt to shoot at the boy actors as well,
and no attack on the stage was complete without a
lengthy dissertation on the necessity for breaking
Mosaic law which was the result of the boy actor
convention. The text which they quoted was:

The woman shall not wear that which pertaineth unto a man, neither shall a man put on a woman's garment: for all that do so are abomination unto the Lord thy God.

(Deut. xxii. 5.)

A perusal of the Puritan attacks on plays and players is a weary business. Plays are 'quite contrary to the word of grace, and sucked out of the devil's teats to nourish us in idolatry, heathenry, and sin,' as Philip Stubbes has it in his *Anatomy of Abuses* (1583), and players are equally damnable. The tergiversating Anthony Munday, a player who joined the Puritan ranks for payment, and who served them as the reformed burglar serves the modern evangelist, wrote *A second and third blast of retraite from plaies and Theaters* (1580) under the name of Anglophile Eutho, and in his charity refers to the boy actors thus:

When I see by them yong boies, inclining of themselues vnto wickednes, trained vp in filthie speeches, vnnatural and vnseemlie gestures, to be brought vp by these Schoole-masters in bawderie, and in idlenes, I cannot chuse but with teares and griefe of hart lament.

This passage gives a brief and distorted glimpse of the training of the boys, and hints at a side of their lives which Stubbes attacks more directly when he says:

. . . Then, these goodly pageants being done euery mate sorts to his mate, euery one bringes another homeward of their way verye freendly, and in their secret conclaues (couertly) they play the *Sodomits*, or worse.

The chief Puritan objection to a play merely as a play was that it was an untruth, and so harmful to public morality. Gosson, in *Playes confuted*, invokes Aristotle as an authority in his cause:

In Stage Playes for a boy to put one the attyre, the
gesture, the passions of a woman; for a meane person to
take vpon him the title of a Prince with counterfeit porte,
and traine, is by outward signes to shew them selues otherwise then they are, and so with in the compasse of a lye,
which by Aristotles iudgement is naught of it selfe and to
be fledde.

(p. 197.)

To Gosson, and to the Puritans who used the same
argument (for they were wonderfully repetitious),
Thomas Heywood made a mild reply in *An Apology
for Actors* (1608), speaking thus:

To see our youths attired in the habit of women, who
knowes not what their intents be? who cannot distinguish
them by their names, assuredly knowing they are but to
represent such a lady, at such a tyme appoynted?

As in all such controversies the contestants did not
read each other's works to be convinced, but only to
gather fresh faggots for a new fire of their own.   The
modern reader must allow that for mildness the players
far exceed the zealots.   Their strong point was not
pamphleteering, but acting, and in many contemporary
plays the Puritans and their arguments are made
popular laughing-stocks.   Ben Jonson made ribald
fun of the Puritan insistence upon the letter of Mosaic
law in the fifth Act of *Bartholomew Fair* (1614).   The
fanatical Rabbi Zeal-of-the-Land Busy attacks a puppet
show with cries of 'Down with Dagon'; bidden to
dispute the matter with the puppet Dionysius he runs
through all the main Puritan points against the stage
and concludes thus:

Busy. Yes, and my main argument against you is, that you

are an abomination: for the male, among you, putteth on the apparel of the female, and the female of the male.

Dion. You lie, you lie, you lie abominably.

Cokes. Good, by my troth, he has given him the lie thrice.

Dion. It is your old ſtale argument againſt the players, but it will not hold againſt the puppets; for we have neither male nor female amongſt us.   And that thou may'ſt see, if thou wilt, like a malicious purblind zeal as thou art.

[Takes up his garment.]

Edg. By my faith, there he has answer'd you, friend, a plain demonſtration.

Dion. Nay I 'll prove, againſt e'er a rabbin of them all, that my ſtanding is as lawful as his; that I speak by inspiration, as well as he; that I have as little to do with learning as he; and do scorn her helps as much as he.

Busy. I am confuted, the cause hath failed me.

The Puritans, like so many of their descendants, were convinced that the playhouse was a hotbed of vice, and nothing would persuade them otherwise. Some of their moſt malignant attacks were directed againſt the male actors of women's roles, whom they accused directly of homosexuality.   A full consideration of this aspect of the Puritan attacks would be an unprofitable task in this volume, but in order that the reader may gain some notion of this particular prejudice againſt the boy actors a few examples muſt be given.   These have been taken from William Prynne's *Hiſtrio-maſtix, The Player's Scourge or Actors Tragedie* (1632), a fat book of more than a thousand pages, which forms an admirable compilation of all the Puritan arguments againſt the theatre.   The work is a classic of abuse and a monument to the misplaced scholarship and zeal of its author.   Unluckily for Prynne he referred to women actors as 'notorious

whores,' meaning a group of French actresses who had
appeared at Blackfriars in 1629; the reference was
taken to apply to Queen Henrietta Maria and her
ladies who were about to perform a pastoral at White-
hall.   She made a Star Chamber matter of it, and poor
Prynne was fined £5,000, set in the pillory, shorn of
his ears, branded, and imprisoned for life.   The S. L.
on his cheeks he construed as *Stigmata Laudis*, and bore
his punishment bravely; it is pleasant to know that the
life-sentence was revoked by the Parliament of the
Commonwealth, for although Prynne was a small-
souled and cantankerous zealot with a maggot about
homosexuality, he was a courageous fighter and a
master of invective.

Prynne's first groan is the familiar one that the
theatre attracted greater numbers than the Church,
which no doubt it did, being in many ways a more
attractive institution; he was not himself a playgoer
and describes his slight experience in the playhouse
thus:

. . . For having upon my first arrivall in London, heard
and seene foure severall Playes (to which the pressing
importunity of some ill acquaintance drew me whiles I was
yet a novice) such wickednes, such lewdnes as then made my
penitent heart to loath, my conscience to abhorre all Stage-
playes ever since.

Prynne thought it shameful to apprentice boys to the
profession of a player; their own inclinations were
sufficient to damn them without being exposed to the
lure of the stage.   Thus he wails:

*Pitty is it to consider, how many ingenuous, Witty, comely
youthes, devoted unto God in baptisme, to whom they owe*

themselves, their service; are oft-times by their gracelesse
Parents, even wholy consecrated to the Stage (the *Divels
Chappell*, as the Fathers phrase it) where they are trained up
in the *Schoole of Vice*, the Play-house, (as if their natures were
not prone enough to sinne, unless they had the help of art
to backe them) to the very excesse of all effeminacy, to act
those womanish, whorish parts, which Pagans would even
blush to personate.

(p. 171.)

Authority of all kinds was victuals and drink to Prynne,
and every page of *Histrio-mastix* has a dark frame of
small print referring the reader to the sources of his
information.   He quotes Cyprian's *Epistles* at length,
in his attack on the system of training boys up to the
stage:

And in another Epistle of his, he writes to *Eucratius to
Excommunicate a Player who did traine up Boyes for the Stage, for
that he taught them against the expresse instruction of God himselfe,
how a male might be effeminated into a female, how their sex might
be changed by Art, that so the divell who defiles God's workeman-
ship, might be pleased by the offences of a depraved and effeminated
body.   I think it will not stand with the Majestie of God, nor the
discipline of the Gospel, that the modestie and honour of the Church
should be polluted with such a filthy and infamous contagion.   For
since men are prohibited with law to put on a woman's garment, and
such who doe it are adjudged accursed.   How much more greater a
sinne is it, not onely to put on woman's apparell, but likewise to
expresse obscene, effeminate and womanish gestures, by the skill or
tutorship of an unchaste Art? . . . One being a Youth (writes
Saint Chrysostome) combes back his haire, and effeminating nature
with his visage, his apparell, his gesture, and the like, strives to
represent the person of a tender virgin. . . .*

The evil of such a practice, to Prynne's mind, was that
it made the male actor of woman's parts unduly
attractive to the audience and to his associates, and in

this he is nearer to the truth of the matter than those who dismiss such a suggestion as ridiculous or unlikely on one ground or another.   Whoever has been in charge of a play presented at a boy's school will not be too ready to dismiss as nonsense this charge of Prynne's:

> Lastly, this putting on of woman's array (especially to act a lascivious, amorous, whorish, Love-sicke Play upon the Stage, must needs be sinfull, yea abominable: *because it not onely excites many adulterous filthy lusts, both in the Actors and Spectators; and drawes them on both to contemplative and actuall lewdnesse,* . . . which is evill, but likewise *instigates them to selfe-pollution,* (*a sinne for which* Onan *was destroyed*): *and to that unnaturall Sodomiticall sinne of uncleanesse, to which the reprobate Gentiles were given over;* (*a* sinne *not once to be named,* much lesse then practised *among Christians*;)
>
> (p. 208.)

It has always been the ill-fortune of the stage and the ballet, because one of their greatest charms is the deliberate display of beauty, to attract both among their practitioners and their audience many people whose fineness of artistic appreciation is not balanced by common serenity of soul, and who bring opprobrium upon the arts which they affect by the obliquity of their moral outlook.   Gifted they may be but, human nature being what it is, the singularity of their conduct in private life attracts more notice than their contributions to art and blinds many people with strong morals but slight aesthetic sense to their genuine worth.   There have been homosexuals of genius, though the assumption popular among their fellows that their greatness was a result of their peculiarity is

the grossest self-flattery; the majority are superficial
folk of no great importance either for good or evil,
but their company is a danger to the weak artist who
mistakes the rarefied atmosphere of their circle for the
thin air of Olympus, and their very presence is a thorn
in the flesh of the many who pride themselves, for lack
of any other source of pride, on their normality. To
a man like Prynne they were anathema, and the picture
which he paints is not an edifying one. He repeats
Stubbes's charge:

Yea witnes . . . M. *Stubs*, his *Anatomy of Abuses* p. 205
where he affirmes, *that Players and Play-haunters in their secret
conclaves play the Sodomites:* together with *some moderne
examples of such, who have been desperately enamored with Players
Boyes thus clad in woman's apparell, so farre as to solicite them by
words, by Letters, even actually to abuse them.*

and it is particularly painful for the present author to
foul his own nest, however retroactively, by tran-
scribing the note which Prynne makes on this passage:

This I have heard credibly reported of a Scholler of
Bayliol Colledge and I doubt not but it may be verified of
divers others.

Prynne's stories of the players' life lose nothing in
the telling, and he quotes old and new works for whatever support they may offer. Cyprian's tenth Epistle
to Eucratio lends weight to his accusation:

The more than Sodomiticall uncleannesse of Players lives,
the father thus decyphers. *O* (writes he) *that those couldest in
that sublime watch-tower insinuate thine eyes into these Players
secrets; or set open the closed dores of their bed-chambers, and bring
all their innermost hidden Cels into the conscience of theire eyes;
Thou shouldest then see that which is even a very sinne to see: thou*

mighteſt behold that, which these groaning under the burthen of their
vices, deny that they have committed, and yet haſten to commit: men
rush on men with outrageous luſts.   (p. 235.)

This evil, Prynne feared, was liable to spread from the
players to the ſpectators; the attractions of the players
were too ſtrong an enticement; again he quotes
Cyprian (*De ſpectaculis lib.*):

Yea, men (writes he in another place) *are unmanned on the*
Stage: all the honour and vigour of their sex is effeminated with the
shame, the dishoneſty of an unsinued body. He who is moſt
womanish and beſt resembles the female sex, gives beſt content. The
more criminous, the more applauded is he; and by how much the
more obscene he is, the more skilfull is he accounted. What cannot
he perswade who is such a one?

                                                    (p. 168.)

In his opinion the players were a danger to the manli-
ness of the nation, and he thought he saw signs of
degeneracy in the exuberance of the later Renaissance.
He groans:

For whence is it *that many of our Gentry are lately degenerated*
into a more than Sardanapalian effeminacy; that they are now so
fantaſtique in their apparell, so womannish in their frizled
Periwigs, Love-lockes, and long effeminate pouldred
pounced haire; so mimicall in their geſtures; so effeminate in
their lives; so Player-like in their deportment, so amorous
in their embracements; so unmanly, degenerous and un-
English (if I may so speake) in their whole conversation; is
it not principally from their resort to Playes, to Masques,
and such like antique, apish Paſtimes, the very Schooles to
traine them up in all effeminacy, and fantaſtique folly?
undoubtedly it is.

It is to be wondered if Prynne considered himself the
type of all that was 'English.'

The theatre as seen through Prynne's eyes is a very

c

sink of iniquity, and the male actors of women's roles seem to be one of its worst features. Fortunately the judgment of this later age will be less prejudiced than was his; even a Puritan cannot make smoke without fire, however, and the conservative reader will gather from the violence of the Puritan attack that the pre-Restoration theatre was a very gay place, and that the boy actors were not lacking in spirit, which may often have created situations disagreeable to the conventional moralist of any age.

Boys continued to play women's parts in all plays until the theatres were closed, and when plays became popular after the Restoration they took up their work again. King Charles, however, had become accustomed to actresses abroad and suggested that women should appear on the English stage; he made some claim that he did so in the interests of morality, and in deference to the Puritan accusations against the boy actors. In view of the character of that monarch the concern he showed in this matter may be considered ironical, for the actresses who flourished under him created a scandal which has never been equalled in the British theatre. It has not been possible to decide which actress was the first to appear on the English stage, but the best claim is that of Mrs Margaret Hughes, the mistress of Prince Rupert, who appeared as Desdemona in *The More of Venice* on Saturday, 8th December 1660. To mark the occasion a prologue was written by Thomas Jordan containing these lines:

I come, unknown to any of the rest,
To tell you news: I saw the lady drest:

The woman plays to-day; miſtake me not;
No man in gown, or Page in petty-coat;
        . . . In this reforming age
We have intents to civilize the Stage.
Our women are defeſtive, and so siz'd
You 'd think they were some of the Guard disguiz'd
For (to speak truth) men aſt, that are between
Forty and fifty, wenches of fifteen;
With bone ſo large, and nerve so incomplyant,
When you call Desdemona, enter Giant.
                  (*A Royal Arbor of Loyal Poesie*, 1664.)

It is likely that in this prologue the case againſt the male aſtors of women's parts is exaggerated in order to throw into relief the superior charms of Mrs Hughes; it is probable also that the Commonwealth had interrupted the training of boy aſtors to such an extent that many of the new ones were unsatisfaſtory, and those who had been popular before the closing of the theatres were too old for their work. There were a few experienced ones, however, who were much admired, notably Edward Kynaſton. Colley Cibber remembered him, and in his *Apology* (1740) writes thus of him:

In a word Kynaſton at that time was so beautiful a Youth, that the Ladies of Quality prided themselves in taking him with them in their coaches to *Hyde-Park*, in his *T*heatrical *H*abit after the *P*lay; which in those Days they might have sufficient time to do, because Plays then were us'd to begin at four a-*C*lock The Hour that people of the same Rank are now going to Dinner. Of this truth, I had the curiosity to enquire, and had it confirmed from his own mouth, in his advanced age.

                            (Chap. V.)

Pepys, too, saw Kynaſton and admired him; in his

Diary for Monday, 7th January 1660/1, when Kynaston was about twenty years old, he records a performance of Jonson's *Epicœne*:

> Among other things here, Kinaston, the boy, had the good turn to appear in three shapes: first as a poor woman in ordinary clothes, to please Morose; then in fine clothes as a gallant, and in them was clearly the prettiest woman in the whole house, and lastly as a man; and then likewise did appear the handsomest man in the house.

John Downes has left a eulogy on Kynaston in his *Roscius Anglicanus*, in which he gives some details concerning his performances at the Cock-Pit in Drury Lane in 1659:

> *Mr Kynaston* acted *Arthiope*, in the Unfortunate Lovers; The Princess in the Mad Lover; *Aglaura*, *Ismenia*, in the Maid in the Mill; and several other Women's Parts; he being then very young made a Compleat female Stage Beauty, performing his Parts so well, especially *Arthiope* and Aglaura, being Parts greatly moving Compassion and Pity; that it has since been Disputable among the Judicious, whether any Woman that succeeded him so Sensibly touch'd the Audience as he.

Whoever was the first actress to appear, she was quickly followed by others and by 1670 they were acting in all London's theatres. The tradition of the boy actors was lost and, except for Downes and the disputing 'Judicious' to whom he refers, they were not regretted. It has always been fashionable in the theatre to be contemptuous of the usages of the recent past, and the general opinion of playgoers and dramatists seems to have been that the actresses were a great gain to the theatre and that it was surprising that

*Mrs Margaret Hughes, the first of the English actresses :
from a portrait by Sir Peter Lely*

good plays should have been written before there was a Nell Gwyn to grace them. In the succeeding century Montesquieu records that Lord Chesterfield was heard to explain to Queen Caroline that the coarseness and inadequacy of Shakespeare's female characterization was the result of his having only boys to play the women's parts. Critics of Shakespeare during the eighteenth century ignored the point, and those of the nineteenth century mentioned it merely to marvel at the greatness of the dramatist who wrote great parts for actresses when there were none in his theatre. No one investigated the history of the boy actors and no one thought of them except as a peculiarity of the unsatisfactory Elizabethan playhouse. A story which first appeared in Cibber's *Apology*, about a performance of *Othello* which was delayed while Desdemona was being shaved, gained great popularity in theatrical circles, and was a favourite witticism of Sir Henry Irving. This attitude persisted until fairly recently, and the following extract represents an opinion still widely held:

In Shakespeare's day boys or men took the part of women and how characters like Lady Macbeth and Desdemona were adequately rendered by youths beggars description. But renderings in such conditions proved popular and satisfactory. Such a fact seems convincing testimony, not to the ability of Elizabethan or Jacobean boys—the nature of boys is a pretty permanent factor in human society—but to the superior imaginative faculty of the adult Elizabethan or Jacobean playgoers, in whom, as in Garrick's time, the needful dramatic illusion was far more easily evoked than it is nowadays.

This quotation is from *Shakespeare and the Modern Stage*

published by no less an authority than Sir Sidney Lee in 1906; he later revised this opinion to the extent of saying that 'boys and young men rendered female roles effectively and without serious injury to the dramatist's conceptions.'

With the exception of William Poel, the founder and director of the Elizabethan Stage Society, no producer or actor-manager in the nineteenth century gave any consideration to the problem presented by the boy actor; Poel was considered to be a visionary and was therefore disregarded except by a small but discerning group. The first writer to attract the notice of the general theatrical and critical world to the importance of the boys in forming Elizabethan dramatic technique was Harley Granville-Barker, who in his prefaces to the *Player's Shakespeare* and in *Prefaces to Shakespeare* gives considerable attention to the matter but, owing to the wide scope of his work, is unable to deal with it exhaustively. The object of this present study is to consider the women's roles in Shakespeare with reference to the potentialities of the boy actor, but before attempting such a task it is necessary to reconstruct as far as possible the training of the boys and to discover their limitations and their special excellences.

There is no evidence that Shakespeare or his contemporaries found the boy actors unsatisfactory interpreters of their work, but there are passages which show that they were well pleased by them. Ben Jonson has a complimentary reference to a contemporary boy actor, Richard Robinson, in Act II, Scene III of *The Devil is an Ass*, as follows:

Meer.   Why this
  Is well! the clothes we have now: but where's this lady?
  If we could get a witty boy now, Engine;
  That were an excellent crack, I could instruct him
  To the true height: For any thing takes this Dottrel.
Eng. Why, sir, your best will be one of the players!
Meer. No, there's no trusting them; they'll talk of it,
  And tell their poets.
Eng.   What if they do! The jest
  Will brook the stage. But there be some of 'em
  Are very honest lads: there's Dickey Robinson,
  A very pretty fellow, and comes often
  To a gentleman's chamber, a friend of mine. We had
  The merriest supper of it there, one night,
  The gentleman's landlady invited him
  To a gossip's feast: now he, sir, brought Dick Robinson,
  Drest like a lawyer's wife, amongst 'em all:
  I lent him clothes.—But to see him behave it,
  And lay the law, and carve and drink unto them,
  And then talk bawdy, and send frolics! O
  It would have burst your buttons, or not left you
  A seam.
Meer.   They say he's an ingenious youth.
Eng. O sir! and dresses himself the best, beyond
  Forty of your very ladies; did you never see him?

Another reference to the skill of the boy actors is
found in the Induction to *The Taming of the Shrew*. The
Lord, who is planning his jest at the expense of
Christopher Sly, calls one of his servants and says:

  Sirrah, go you to Barthol'mew my page
  And see him dressed in all suits like a lady:
  That done, conduct him to the drunkard's chamber
  And call him 'madam,' do him obeisance.
  Tell him from me, as he will win my love,
  He bear himself with honourable action,
  Such as he hath observed in noble ladies
  Unto their lords, by them accomplished:

Such duty to the drunkard let him do
With soft low tongue and lowly courtesy,
And say, 'What is 't your honour will command,
Wherein your lady and your humble wife
May show her duty, and make known her love?'
And then with kind embracements, tempting kisses,
And with declining head into his bosom,
Bid him shed tears, as being overjoy'd
To see her noble lord restor'd to health,
Who for this seven years hath esteemed him
No better than a poor and loathesome beggar:
And if the boy have not a woman's gift
To rain a shower of commanded tears,
An onion will do well for such a shift,
Which in a napkin (being close convey'd)
Shall in despite enforce a watery eye.
See this dispatch'd with all the haste thou canst
Anon I 'll give thee more instructions.
I know the boy will well usurp the grace,
Voice, gait, and action of a gentlewoman.

There is certainly no doubt here of the capability of
the boy actor to present the outward semblance of
a woman, but acting is more than mimicry, and doubt
might reasonably be entertained as to the boy's
capacity to express the emotions demanded of such a
character as Rosalind or Juliet, and at this point it is
necessary to consider Sir Sidney Lee's remark that 'the
nature of boys is a pretty permanent factor in human
society.' It is fruitless to dispute about the essential
nature of any group of human beings, but it must be
clear to any one who will trouble to examine their
place in social history that boys are as much subject to
the *Zeitgeist* as adults and that their characteristics are
generally those which are expected of them by the age
in which they live. It is true that many boys are

characterized by an oafishness which their elders find agreeable because it makes the boys less troublesome than if they were acute. During the latter half of the nineteenth century, and even yet in many circles, the influence of public school education and the spirit of the age tended to make boys conventional and scornful of vigorous expressions of emotion, exalting intellectual stagnation and Red Indian stoicism above all other virtues. Some boys, however, have always been intelligent, self-reliant, and capable of extremes of virtue and vice far beyond the reach of the majority of their elders, and in the reigns of Elizabeth and James I there were many opportunities for these lads to make a place for themselves, as it was not then fashionable for youth to be a period of ignorance and ineptitude. The time set a high value on boldness, passion, and individuality, and the boys of the time began to develop these qualities at an early age, and never thought of stifling them lest their spiritual vigour should give offence. Adolescence is always a period of emotional conflicts, and these are not so superficial as dispassionate or stupid observers care to think. There are surprising depths of emotion to be found in boys, and the Elizabethans were under no obligation to keep it rigorously under control. Shakespeare puts a significant speech into the mouth of Rosalind:

> . . . at which time would I, being but a moonish youth, grieve, be effeminate, changeable, longing, and liking, proud, fantastical, apish, shallow, inconstant, full of tears, full of smiles; for every passion something, and for no

passion truly any thing; as boys and women are for the most part cattle of this colour.

(*As You Like It*, Act III, Sc. ii, ll. 396–402.)

There need be no doubt that the Elizabethan boy-actors had at their command a plentiful supply of superficial emotion of the type which can so readily be converted into the material of acting, and doubtless the life of the theatre and the adulation which success would bring developed their capacities to the full. The age was one of emotional friendships of a sort no longer common and difficult to imagine, and the relation between Antonio and Bassanio was far more real to the Elizabethans than it can be to us. Similarly the friendship which existed between the boy actors and the poets or the noblemen who patronized the theatre may well have been of an intensity to alarm a Puritan without having any smack of sin to the less inhibited players. The nature of boys, to which Sir Sidney Lee refers, contains abilities for hero-worship, affection, and consequently coquetry, which probably do less harm when they are given expression than when they are bottled up. It is not necessary to discuss at length the justice of the Puritan charges of homosexuality against the players and the boy actors; doubtless there were some grounds for them and certainly it was inevitable that boys brought up in an artistic and somewhat raffish atmosphere should fall as far short of the Puritan ideal of conduct as they soared above the Puritan understanding of the very mixed business of living. To examine too deeply into the affairs of any class of society is to puddle in dirty water at last, and the queasy should refrain from doing so.

The boys had superficial emotion in plenty, and that over a surprising range, but on the stage, as in all arts, experience of life gives depth and understanding to the artists' work, and superficial emotion is not enough to make an actor of first-rate ability. The object of this study is to demonstrate the way in which the Shakespearian women's roles are written to exploit fully the capacity of the boy actors for easy and febrile emotion *
without demanding the greater range of passion which only time and experience can bring.

The training of the boys by their masters and by the poets who produced their plays was exhaustive, and the importance of this personal instruction by the author should not be overlooked. Jonson mentions the custom whereby the poet trains his actors (in this case children in the Induction to *Cynthia's Revels*), and, in *Roscius Anglicanus*, Downes refers to the tradition of acting *Hamlet* handed down from Taylor of the Blackfriars Company, who was 'Instructed by the Author Mr Shakespeur'; the chronology of this latter statement casts doubt on Taylor's claim, but does not alter the tradition that Shakespeare, like other practical dramatists of the time, trained his own players. The style of acting used by the Elizabethans may be reconstructed from the drama of the time, and it is obvious that an elaborate technique of delivery and pantomime was necessary in order to perform to the satisfaction of the audiences who attended the public playhouses. They expected the acting to be full-blooded and exciting, and they wanted passion presented in brilliant colours. Hamlet was probably representative of his time in his appreciation of a passionate speech for its own sake, without reference to its context. The Elizabethans delighted in feats of virtuosity, and their desire was willingly gratified by their actors. The tradition of acting was that handed down from the morality plays, with their roaring Vice, and of the miracles, in which Herod raged and stormed before an audience filled with delicious terror. There are frequent references to the actor's expansive gestures and his strutting, stamping walk. Shakespeare makes a striking reference to this mannerism in *Troilus and Cressida*, thus:

> . . . like a strutting player, whose conceit
> Lies in his hamstring, and doth think it rich
> To hear the wooden dialogue and sound
> 'Twixt his stretch'd footing and the scaffoldage.
> (Act I, Sc. III, ll. 153–6.)

Facial expression, too, appears to have played a very important part in acting, and there are many comments upon it: in *The Returne from Pernassus*, Act IV, Kempe gives an exhibition of his skill in pulling faces, and there is a lesson in face-making in the second Act of *Cynthia's Revels*, which must have been highly entertaining to see. There are references to facial expression in many of Shakespeare's plays, perhaps the best-known being Hamlet's admonishment to the villain in The Murder of Gonzago:

> . . . pox, leave thy damnable faces, and begin.
> (Act III, Sc. II, ll. 266–7.)

Elizabethan actors were accomplished dancers. This wood-cut from ' Kempes Nine Daies Wonder' (1600) shows Shakespeare's original Dogberry, Will Kempe, performing a 'jig'

The player here, representing one of his own kind within a play, would doubtless exaggerate the characteristics of his art and stamp and mouth horribly.

The reasons for this extravagance in Elizabethan acting are not difficult to discover. Elizabethan manners were less restrained than those of later days, and the actor who wished to hold the mirror up to nature had to copy and exaggerate the common standards of behaviour; exaggerate he must, for no audience will watch an actor who is really behaving as he would off the stage, and even the acting of the naturalistic school is carefully studied. Acting in the open air, on a bare stage, and as there was no other means of focusing the attention of the spectators on the stage, the actor had to make himself interesting, and at the beginning of the play at least he would have to strut and gesticulate and shout his lines in order to gain the necessary domination over an audience which was probably ill-mannered and ready to mock him if he failed to please. The violence of the acting would make necessary a similar violence of delivery, and Shakespeare has more than one reference to the bellowings of the actor who affected 'Ercles' vein.'

The excessive violence of the Elizabethan actor in such a part as Tamburlaine must have been tempered with delicacy upon occasion, for it is impossible to shout and stamp through *Love's Labour's Lost* or *A Midsummer Night's Dream*. Such plays as these make their own demands of graceful movement and beautiful speech, which were of first importance to the comedian. Rapidity of delivery was characteristic of the Elizabethan stage, where, in order to complete a five-act tragedy near to the two hours customary for the ordinary performance, the actors had to play on and to the lines, without pauses for effective 'silent business'; rapidity of speech without skill would certainly have provoked those temperamental audiences to bitter comment. The general tendency of Elizabethan acting was toward magnificence of appearance and gesture, and rapid, athletic speech. The great actor was a virtuoso and the audience expected a brilliant display of his powers.

Acting of this sort cannot be described without using expressions which could not be applied to a modern actor except in derogation. There is no doubt, however, that it was magnificent and stirring, for a strutting walk and a stentorian delivery and those formal gestures which the platform stage demanded, if backed up by a finely poetic spirit and an egregious personality, would give the actor a personal gorgeousness and transcendency admirably suited to great poetic drama. The modern tendency to attempt to give greater 'reality' to Shakespeare's heroes and heroines by playing them as young ladies and gentlemen with the manners and speech of the suburban tennis-court can only produce vulgarity in roles which were never meant to be played in that way. The greatest 'reality' is achieved in Shakespeare by those actors who are able to reach magnificence in technique and conception and can present a great man in his full and blazing colours, without attempting to give him 'reality' by stamping him as a dictator, or a gun-man, or in some other way displaying that misplaced ingenuity which must always be imposing a meretriciously modern guise upon a timeless work of art.

The Elizabethan actor, in the words of a book called *The Rich Cabinet Furnished with varietie of excellent discriptions* (1616), was noted for 'dancing, actiuitie, musicke, song, elloqution, abilitie of body, memory, skill of weapon, pregnancy of wit,' and it would be these qualities which his master would seek to instil into the boy actor, although 'pregnancy of wit' would doubtless be a condition of his apprenticeship, as would a well-formed body and a moderately agreeable face. The training in dancing and gesture would be strenuous, for dancers were often required in the plays, and it was a part of the Elizabethan actor's versatility that he should be able to perform a 'jig' (a kind of song-and-dance) when it was required of him. The Elizabethan actor resembled the modern variety entertainer in his ability to do almost anything that would give amusement. Dancing would be a preliminary training for the boy, to make him supple and to give him grace and command over his body. The training in gesture would be exhaustive, for in a theatre where new plays were constantly being presented there would be little time to do more than learn the words of a part and have a few rehearsals, which would give slight opportunity for elaborate training in individual roles. The actor had to have his gestures at his command so that he could produce those which were appropriate without too much reflection. In the formal Elizabethan method of acting this would not be out of the question, and there were no doubt well-worn gestures for contempt, rage, pity, remorse, and all the other emotions, which the audience would quickly accept as symbols of them. The Elizabethan conventions of gesture cannot have been radically unlike those of the Italian *Commedia dell' arte*, whose system of gestures with the body, the limbs, and the hands, and the various expressions of the face, is adequate to express any emotion in any degree of intensity. Readers who wish to study the Italian system closely will find it excellently described in Charles Aubert's *The Art of Pantomime*, an English translation of which was made in 1927: such a study will reveal the remarkable possibilities which these formal gestures have for the expression of emotion.

The boy actor would also be required to spend some time in learning the management of his dress, for the clothes of an Elizabethan lady were always heavy, and the dresses of the players were celebrated for their richness. The long, heavy skirts require skilful management, and when they are rightly used they are in themselves a wonderful instrument of expression; the beauty-loving Elizabethans would be unlikely to overlook the possibilities of those expressive folds. Smaller boys may have worn chopines under cover of their skirts to give themselves height. A boy, when dressed for his part, would seem much taller and more impressive than ordinarily he would, and there can be no doubt that this would form a striking contrast with his appearance of fragility when he was forced by the circumstances of the play to change into his doublet and hose. The uses to which Shakespeare puts this fragility—to excite pity and to give the boy an opportunity of exercising his charm unhampered by the necessity to pretend that he is a woman—are discussed in the subsequent chapters of this study, in connection with the characters to which they apply.

Make-up, too, would do much to create the illusion of beauty. There are frequent condemnatory references to face-painting in the Puritan writings. Philip Stubbes, in *The Anatomy of Abuses*, tells us that:

The Women of England, many of them, use to collour their faces with certaine Oyles, Liquors, Vnguents, & waters made to that end . . .

and doubtless the boy actors did the same. Wigs they certainly wore, and modern actresses share this in common with them—when Rosalind or Julia turns from woman to boy she takes off her wig and wears her own shorter hair. The possession of fair or auburn hair would be as advantageous to a boy then as it is to an actress now, for that was the fashionable colour, Queen Elizabeth being a red-head, and 'second ladies' were dark in contrast.

Fencing would be a necessary part of the boy's training, for the Elizabethans delighted in sword-play on the stage, and every audience would contain many critics who could justly appraise every move in the duels and battle-scenes. The fights in Elizabethan drama were realistic to a dangerous degree and were prolonged in order to give the actors a chance to show their skill and to delight the connoisseurs. Fencing

D

also would give the boy grace and self-control and
consequently the ease of manner on the stage which
would be necessary if he were to play the part of a
great lady.   Gymnastics of many sorts are required in
Elizabethan drama, and the tradition of the actors who
were also tumblers was persistent.   The physical
education of the boy actors would make them strong
and alert and, above all, graceful.   The audiences
accepted them as women without question or thought
of incongruity and Coryate was amazed to see women
act in Venice; he writes in his *Crudeties* (1611) as
follows:

> I saw women acte, a thing that I neuer saw before . . .
> and they performed it with as good a grace, action, gesture,
> and whatsoever conuenient for a Player, as ever I saw any
> masculine Actor.
>
> (p. 247.)

The training of the boys in speech and song was of
the utmost importance in a theatre where declamation
was appreciated for its own sake and where the
women's roles contained long rhetorical and antithetical speeches and soliloquies.   Strength of voice
was necessary to ensure audibility in the open air, but
coarseness had to be avoided, for the Elizabethan
world was deeply sensitive to tone and cadence, and
although many of an audience might be illiterate the
majority had a strong relish for the beauty of the
spoken word.   Critics have made much of Shakespeare's repeated reference to the soft, low voices
of women, but in the theatre this cannot be understood literally.   A well-trained speaking voice has a

resonance and a richness of quality which is pleasing
even when the actual tone of the voice is high, and a
good voice is never strident.   To speak in a soft, low
tone in the open air is to be inaudible, but a well-
trained voice would give precisely the effect of beauty
and careful modulation which is required.

A difficulty encountered by the boy actors would be
the breaking of the voice from treble to bass, which
might begin at any age from twelve onward, and
which would certainly decrease his value as a player of
women's roles.   The break, however, can be controlled, and in a trained voice can be deferred and
concealed for two or three years.   The usual tendency
of boys, when their voices break, is to use the new
bass voice, no matter what strain it may cause, but the
boy actor, whose usefulness to his master and to the
company depended upon his retaining a treble voice,
would have every inducement to preserve it as long
as possible.   Careful training will preserve almost any
boy's voice unbroken for speaking until the age of
seventeen.

In this connection it may be observed that when
their livelihood depends upon it boys still preserve
their voices for some years after the normal time for
the break.   The modern boy actors who play in such
pieces as *Peter Pan* as 'Lost Boys,' or in *Where the
Rainbow Ends*, all use treble or very light tenor voices,
and their ages often range from sixteen to nineteen.
Mr Cuthbert Kelly, whose researches into Elizabethan
and Jacobean music have included not only the music
itself but an inquiry into the voice-training methods of

the time, is of opinion that the boy actors would be able to preserve their voices for singing until sixteen at least, and for speaking until nineteen or twenty. The tone of the singing voice might change from a boy's treble to a 'cathedral alto' or a very high tenor. The extent to which the tone of the speaking voice might change would be greater, but it is probable that with boys who had had so long a training in speaking it would remain sufficiently gentle or womanly until at least nineteen or twenty. The voice both in singing and speaking might become less brilliant but it would not necessarily become harsh or artificial.

There is some reason to believe that the voices of the Elizabethan actors were higher in pitch than those of their modern successors. Most Elizabethans were able to sing after a fashion and the actors were all trained in this art, as songs are frequent in the plays of the time. The scene of revelling in *Twelfth Night* cannot have been the gallimaufry of discordant bawling then that it turns to in most modern productions. An examination of contemporary music which has not been transposed shows that the range of it is great but that the general *tessitura* of the songs is too high to be comfortable for any but exceptional modern singers. Thomas Morley, Robert Jones, William Cornysshe, and particularly Alfonso Ferrabosco, of whom Ben Jonson thought so highly, and who wrote music for so many of his masques, were all composers of music which was popular in the theatres, and most of their songs in the original key require a high voice. If the players then trained their voices upward instead of downward, as is now usually the case, the difference between their voices and those of the boys would be lessened, and it must also be borne in mind that all trained voices have a certain similarity not of pitch but of timbre; the listener is impressed not so much by the pitch of the voice as by its quality, and it is often difficult to distinguish by sound alone between a well-trained man's voice and that of a woman.

While the boys were being trained they made themselves useful about the playhouse by assisting the stage-keeper, running on errands and carrying stools and tobacco-pipes to the stage for the gentlemen who chose to sit there. They would be useful also as figures in a pageant, or as pages in the train of a nobleman and as extra ladies in dances and scenes requiring many players. It is doubtful if they were ever kept by an actor for training alone; they must always have done something to earn a wage, and in those days, when children were expected to work for long hours, there can be no doubt that their training and their minor tasks at the playhouse occupied most of their time. No doubt they enjoyed themselves, and sometimes in surprising ways. In *The Returne from Pernassus* a boy enters to speak the Prologue, but cannot remember his words; in the expressive language of the stage-direction he is *non plus*. Two adult actors then appeal to the audience to excuse him for he has been sitting up all night at cards, and has had no time to sleep upon his part. Three years would do much to develop what talent a boy might have, and with his training in speech and gesture he would, at the age of fifteen, be competent to play important roles very well.

Before turning to the study of the Shakespearian women's roles it is necessary to consider briefly the nature of the dramatic illusion which the Elizabethan theatre provided. The first impression which is received by the student who attempts such a task is one of hopeless confusion of method. The stage is bare and open, and the means of entrance to it are limited, and yet such oddities as individual trees and mossy banks make occasional appearances upon it. The style of acting is formal and exaggerated, yet scenes of wonderfully delicate pathos or comedy are met with in Elizabethan plays. Verse is used to supply the atmosphere of most of the scenes but severed heads and limbs are introduced to give a grisly reality to certain incidents. The Elizabethan stage does not adhere either to the formalism which its limited resources seemed to impose upon it nor does it make a determined effort toward naturalism, but wavers between the two and employs each in turn and both together as the whim of the dramatist dictates. It is extremely likely, however, that this eclectic method of presentation was a strength and not a weakness, and provided a very adaptable medium with which to work. The consistency with which the Victorians, led by Charles Kean, produced Shakespeare's plays on the representational stage served only to disgust the members of his audience who cared for their poetry, and the dreariness of certain recent experiments in which the plays are performed in symbolic illumination in front of a symbolic background are convincing testimony that neither extreme formalism nor extreme realism can do anything but harm to Shakespeare, for both trammel the imagination of the spectators.

When Shakespeare's plays are considered with this mixture of formalism and naturalism in mind, it is striking to observe how many of the scenes in which women appear in prominent roles are cast in the formal mould. The boy actor is given the advantage x of that aloofness which very mannered acting engenders whether in comedy or tragedy; in the presence of very formal and mannered acting the instinct of the audience is to delight in the virtuosity of the players rather than to identify themselves emotionally with the action, and, x although this sort of acting is not greatly appreciated at the moment, the pleasure, whether comic or tragic, which it gives, is second only to that derived from tragic acting of the very first order. For comedy, it is possible to prefer the formal method to the naturalistic one.

It cannot successfully be contended that the art of the boy actors was either wholly formal or realistic. There was a very workmanlike technique behind it, which made the initial task of successfully appearing as a woman an easy matter, but technique alone would not serve to carry a boy through a role like Imogen or Viola. In all his principal women's parts Shakespeare has given the boy actor opportunities to use his own personal charm, which may easily have been consider- x able. He calls upon the boy's stores of emotion, but the means by which the emotion is presented allow the boy to make full use of his mastery of gesture and speech, and to eke out his lack of communicable deep feeling with his technical skill. The ways in which he makes his women's roles suitable for performance by boys without making them subsidiary are many, and the succeeding three chapters of this study will be devoted to a detailed examination of the women of the comedies, the women of the tragedies, and those parts of old women and children which provide unusual features, in an attempt to elucidate them. Such a prospect may perhaps alarm the reader who has no specialist's interest in Shakespeare, and the writer has no hesitation in recommending such a one to skip many passages in the three chapters which follow, reading only those which deal with his favourites among Shakespeare's heroines. It is to be hoped, however, that no one who reads the book in this fashion will take upon himself to condemn the argument, for unless he has read the book thoroughly he cannot fully understand it.

CHAPTER II

The Women's Roles in Shakespeare's Comedies discussed with reference to the Boy Actor

A CONSIDERATION, in detail, of the heroines of the comedies and those waiting gentlewomen and confidantes who are the heroines of the sub-plots will explain not only the mechanics of their own parts but will help to make clear the subsequent study of the heroines of the tragedies. The parts given to the women in the comedies are longer, and although perhaps they are not more important than those of the heroines of the tragedies considered aesthetically, they give more opportunity for the display of the technical proficiency which was the staple of the boy actor's art. The devices used by the playwright to present his female characters in the form most suited to the convention of the boy actor are subtle and elusive, and after an exhaustive search through a few of the plays, there is serious danger of seeing them where they do not exist, and of building an elaborate case upon unsound evidence. This danger has not been avoided by writers who have sought for proofs of Shakespeare's remarkable understanding of women and his lifelike depiction of them, and it would be a pity to repeat the mistake in the present search. There is some evidence, however, which lies in the borderland, and which may seem acceptable to some observers and not to others; although it is difficult to excise personal opinion entirely, where such evidence occurs in this study it will not be too vigorously urged.

The playwright who has to consider the boy actor as one of the conventions and limitations of his theatre might well find comedy a grateful medium of expression, for in comedy the plot, and the situations within the plot, are of first importance, and if he has a sturdy fable his extravagances and laxities of character drawing will be forgiven, or overlooked by his audience. Shakespeare has taken advantage of this with many of his men, but his women are all shown with discretion, almost with caution, so that in their most vigorous passages they are unlikely to commit any artistic indiscretion which will seriously disturb the balance of the play. We have ample evidence in one famous speech [1] of Shakespeare's detestation of the clown who sacrificed the unity of the play to his own vanity, and he took no risk of similar personal exploitation by his boy actors. True, the position of the boys in the company would make any such action on their part much less possible than it would be for a clown of Kempe's reputation, but any one who has had experience on the stage needs no reminder of the thousand tricks and mannerisms by which an actor can force himself upon an audience to the hurt of the play, and one supposes that a boy actor who was permitted by his part to do this would have been encouraged in his evil ways by the audience, a large part of which is always ready to acclaim vulgar self-display as extraordinary talent. This would account for the infrequency in his plays of displays of coyness and that vacillation of will which is supposed to be a distinctively feminine quality, as both these emotional states become, in action, fields for a sort of self-exploitation very dangerous to a young artist and, if unskilfully done, destructive to dramatic illusion.

The singleness of purpose shown by the Shakespearian comedy heroines, besides giving them the charm of stability in a world where the men are as changeable as the weather, makes them, as parts, very easy to act. The boy actor, equipped with his good voice and his training in dancing and gesture, could play them perfectly, and the nature of the parts prevented any display of youthful vanity which was not suitable to them. The youth who prided himself on his ability to show feminine nature in all its moods was curbed by the single-mindedness of the part as it was written. The parts demand technical ability of the very first order, and beyond that, nothing but ease of manner. Effortful acting in these roles is destructive to the fabric of the play; the great flights are left to the men. The comedy heroines are written to be played easily, and to make them easy for boy actors Shakespeare has written them with restraint and a number of devices designed to keep the actor within his technical resources.

Before proceeding to an examination of the comedies it would be well to clarify the meaning of 'effortful acting,' as it is used here. The part of a young woman in a comedy cannot be played in a slovenly or an abstracted fashion, or it will injure the play. The boy actor must have his wits about him and play vigorously, and in some passages even strenuously, but if he allows himself, through faulty technique, to try his powers too high and to attempt to put into his part more emotion or action than it is designed to take he will inevitably find himself tearing a passion to tatters and nullifying the effectiveness of his part by over-acting. The heroines of Shakespearian comedy are so written that they are well within the scope of a highly trained boy actor and the dangers of this inartistic over-acting are slight.

The discussion of the comedies which follows considers them in a roughly chronological order, and the particular problem of each is treated under its own heading, for the sake of convenience in reference. The sections are not completely independent, however, as an attempt to make them so would swell the book with needless repetition.

THE COMEDY OF ERRORS

In *The Comedy of Errors* the plot is of more importance than the characters, and neither Adriana nor Luciana is more than a Plautian lay-figure. In the first scene in which we see them [2] they are evenly matched, speaking in couplets that tell us nothing of themselves, and which demand no more than competent delivery. In the following scene Adriana has a speech of thirty-two lines, in which no sort of character is established other than the stock one of the wronged wife. Nevertheless, the speech is written with a fine flow of language that makes it effective in delivery. The formal nature of the comedy is reflected in the formality of the dialogue, and the love-scene between Luciana and Antipholus of Syracuse [3] is a sort of poetic duet, designed to be an interlude in the midst of the scenes of broad comedy. Such character as the two women have is shown in accidental touches, as when Adriana says of her supposed husband:

Ah, but I think him better than I say
  And yet would herein others' eyes were worse.
Far from her nest the lapwing cries away: [4]
  My heart prays for him, though my tongue do curse.

It is interesting to notice that the Courtesan is a mere puppet, a clear proof that Shakespeare was more interested in the rapid development of his plot than in character, as he never draws another courtesan who is not well characterized.

THE TAMING OF THE SHREW

In *The Taming of the Shrew* the women's parts are drawn on a larger and, comparatively, more realistic scale, and in the first scene we meet with a device which Shakespeare used lavishly in his early comedies, and used to some extent in all his plays. This is the establishment of a character by means of report, or by comment in asides given to other characters. Here Katharine and Bianca enter with their father and the suitors Gremio and Hortensio; in Gremio's first speech [5] there is a strong hint as to Katharine's character, which she immediately ratifies by a display of ill-nature. In the same way a key to Bianca's nature is given [6] by the watching Lucentio, and her praise is taken up by her father [7] when she leaves the stage. Gremio and Hortensio, left, as they think, alone, continue with a passage [8] which has no other justification than that it adds to the impression we have already received of the two sisters, and when these two are gone Lucentio's declaration of love continues the theme. In the following scene [9], the first in which Petruchio appears, the character already established for Katharine is continued by suggestion and implication until the impression of her shrewishness is stronger than if both scenes had been devoted entirely to displays of her evil temper. Neither Katharine nor Bianca make any really important appearance until the beginning of the second Act, by which time the audience knows precisely what it may expect of them, although Gremio, Hortensio, and even Petruchio are still capable of surprising the spectator who is unfamiliar with the play.

In this respect it is interesting to compare Shakespeare's elaborate building up of the character of Katharine with the simplicity of her introduction in the old and comparatively crude play which was his source. In this, *The Taming of a Shrew*, Polidor refers to her thus:

> And he that hath her shall be fettred so
> As good be wedded to the Diuell him selfe
> For such a skould as she did never live.

Later in the play he calls her 'this Devilish skould.'

Having taken such pains to establish Katharine's

shrewishness, which is the pivot upon which the
mechanics of the plot revolves, it would be dis-
appointing to the audience if some concrete display
of it were denied them, but there are obvious difficulties in a scene of violence entrusted to a boy-actor, ✗
if he is to play it with a man, for in an attempt to get
the best of the scene he may over-act, and so coarsen
the character and deprive it of its charm.   This difficulty is avoided [10] by introducing a scene of violence
between the two women, and it is possible for Katharine to domineer over Bianca and beat her without
exercising too much effort and without turning from
a shrew into a virago, and further evidence of her
shrewishness is given when Hortensio enters with a
vivid tale of how Katharine broke the lute over his
head [11].   The actual wooing has almost no violent
action in it: Katharine cuffs Petruchio once, and otherwise the conflict between them is one of wits, and,
when acted, his bantering tone enhances her fierceness
until an impression is created quite different from the
brawling that might be expected.   It is interesting
throughout the play to notice how much Katharine
derives from the other characters.   When her new-
wedded lord says to her, after their wedding:

Nay, look not big, nor stamp, nor stare, nor fret. [12]

his words lend a significance to her action which would
be difficult to give to it in any other way.   Shakespeare, who need not fear that an actor sufficiently
competent to play Petruchio would bungle so simple
a piece of bluster, allows him to throw the trenchers

and the meat about the stage and thereby gives him an advantage over Katharine in the eyes of the audience, who are always pleased by a realistic display of temper.

The play is interesting in a study of this kind because it depends for its effectiveness on the convincing portrayal of a single characteristic in the principal female role. Bianca and the Widow are easy to act. Katharine is not easy, and the play is so written as to spare the boy who played the part anything which might be beyond his powers. The weight of the play, from an acting point of view, lies on Petruchio from whom Katharine derives continually, as the action is centred round her rebellion against his domineering ways; unless he is a sufficiently good actor to provide a strong Petruchio against whom to rebel, Katharine must fail, for her part by itself is not sufficiently interesting to hold the attention of an audience.

THE TWO GENTLEMEN OF VERONA

There is a striking correspondence between the scene in *The Two Gentlemen of Verona* in which Julia and Lucetta are first shown to the audience [13] and the first sight of Portia and Nerissa in *The Merchant of Venice*. In both plays the heroine is discovered with her confidante discussing the lovers who seek her hand. At the risk of labouring the obvious it may be well here to consider briefly the convention of character which governs the heroine of Elizabethan drama. Audiences did not expect complexity of character in the heroine of comedy and they knew before the play began that she was to be beautiful, accomplished, and of more than human fidelity. These introductory scenes gave necessary information for the completion of her character, for they indicated her social position, showed clearly whether she was or was not enjoying good fortune, and allowed the boy actor to impress the figure and character of his part upon the audience before anything was demanded of him in the way of action. A similar scene is written for Rosalind and Celia [14], and the scene between Viola and the Sea Captain [15], although it differs from the other three in form, is very like them in content, and while on the stage it gives a strong impression of action it is really as static as any of the others. This method of introducing the heroine would become monotonous if used often, but the same effect is gained in other ways in all the comedies. At no time does Shakespeare allow his heroine to enter the action of the play before the audience knows what it may expect of her and has a very clear idea of who and what she is.

An interesting point of technique is illustrated in the lines spoken by Julia when she has torn Proteus's letter [16]. The emotion in the speech seems genuine enough, but the expression of it is formal and conceited. This would be entirely favourable to the art of a boy-actor of competent technique, for the elaboration and formalization of the emotion of the girl who regrets having torn her lover's letter makes it possible to express it in formal and beautiful gesture and intonation, and an impression of beauty and sincerity would be given to the audience by a purely technical

E

means. How much more restrained in expression are the later soliloquies [17], when Julia compares her beauty with that of Silvia. What can explain the disparity between the two, and the different means used to evoke a strong romantic feeling? In the first soliloquy the boy actor is asked to present a highly bred and sensitive lady, and he is given a speech which demands all his skill in elocution and gesture to give it adequate expression. In the later soliloquies he is representing a lady dressed as a page, and while this bars him from too great a dependence upon elaborate gesture, it allows him to express, with a certain amount of nature, a simple emotion. There can be no doubt that the elaborate and rich dresses worn by the boy actors influenced their technique greatly, for considerable skill is required to carry such a costume gracefully and to make the most use of its lines, particularly those of the large full skirts; such a costume favours a rather portentous style of acting, as the wearer must exaggerate his every movement in order to give it a significance in keeping with his dress. The necessity for this elaboration of gesture and speech vanishes when the boy actor appears in his doublet and hose, and would serve only to make him ridiculous in such a costume. He has the advantage, however, that in his male garments he may successfully attempt a certain naturalism in his acting which is a very good method when applied to such wistful passages as this one. In the scene of which this soliloquy is the conclusion Silvia is sympathetically drawn, but in performance the concern of the audience would be all for

Julia, not only because of the pathos of her lines, but because of the pathos of her appearance. Moving upon a stage in which the other boys were elaborately dressed as women and the men considerably bigger than himself, the boy Julia would present a frail and forlorn appearance, the appeal of which to the audience should not be underestimated.

LOVE'S LABOUR'S LOST *and* A MIDSUMMER NIGHT'S DREAM

Love's Labour's Lost and *A Midsummer Night's Dream* do not present any unusual features in the treatment of the women's roles, and these are well within the range of any competent boy actor. It is interesting, however, to note the references which the women in these plays make to their own beauty. In the first of the two the Princess says, perhaps a little ungraciously, in reply to Boyet's compliment:

Good Lord Boyet, my beauty, though but mean, [18]
Needs not the painted flourish of your praise.

and later [19] she makes her beauty the ground for half a dozen witticisms with the forester. In the second of these two plays Hermia and Helena are both complacent on the subject of their attractions before the magic of the forest possesses them [20]. It seems to have been permissible under the boy-actor convention for the women in the plays to make serious and jocose reference to their own beauty, and it cannot be argued that this was necessary in order to give an illusion of beauty, for there is no reason why the boy actor, when dressed and painted, should not have given a very real appearance of beauty. This seems to have been a peculiarity of the stage before the advent of women upon it, for in plays written after the Restoration such references are few, and almost never intended to be taken seriously. Certainly this naïve self-praise is not objectionable in the Shakespearian heroine, but in roles more realistically conceived it might easily become so.

Both *Love's Labour's Lost* and *A Midsummer Night's Dream* are highly conventional, but there can be no doubt as to which is the more attractive play. In the first the women are not carefully differentiated, and as long as they are acted with charm the wit of the lines is sufficient to make them theatrically effective. But in the second play Helena and Hermia present, in performance, a marked contrast. One is tall and fair, the other dark and small; the first is timid and given to self-pity, the second self-willed and sharp-tongued; no great strain, however, is put upon the ability of the boy who plays either part. The characters of the lovers are written in a high-comedy convention which restricts their opportunity for emotional display. Their love-making and their quarrelling are done in beautifully cadenced verse. Tenderness is allowed them, it is true, but it is a stylized tenderness, and the scene in which Hermia and Lysander go to sleep in the wood, protesting their love, has the formal beauty of a dance [21]. Hermia's speech when she awakes to find her lover gone [22] is a piece of bravura which could only suffer by too realistic a performance, but which would have a considerable charm if performed as a 'set' piece, as would Helena's unhappy soliloquy earlier in the play [23].

THE MERCHANT OF VENICE

The means of establishing the character of a comedy heroine which were used so lavishly in *The Taming of the Shrew* are employed with greater subtlety in the service of Portia, and the fine poetic passage in which Bassanio describes her [24] precedes her first entrance by no more than a minute. The effect of this preparatory speech cannot be judged as readily in reading the play as in watching it or, better still, assisting in the production of it. Portia is presented to the audience in Bassanio's eulogy with more beauty of character than any actor could hope to establish in the minds of the audience at once, or in the course of several scenes, and almost immediately afterward Portia and Nerissa appear and engage in a dialogue in which Portia, having all the best lines, firmly imposes herself upon the audience as a delightful and witty person. Some of her wit is of a kind which impresses less by its charm and lightness than by the neatness of its expression; but it has the virtue of speaking well, and a boy actor, a part of whose craft was a rapid and distinguished elocution, would make lovely music of the antithetical passage which runs:

If to do were as easy as to know what were good to do, chapels had been churches, and poor men's cottages princes' palaces; it is a good divine that follows his own instructions,

I can easier teach twenty what were good to be done, than to be one of the twenty to follow mine own teaching: the brain may devise laws for the blood, but a hot temper leaps o'er a cold decree, such a hare is madness the youth, to skip o'er the meshes of good counsel the cripple; but this reasoning is not in the fashion to choose me a husband.— O me, the word 'choose'!

The rhythm of such passages as this demands a more studied delivery than the naturalistic school of acting can give it.   She next appears with Morocco, who is trying his luck in the casket lottery, and in the second scene, in which he makes a choice [25], his meditative speech contains another long passage in praise of Portia, and by this time the audience, who have seen a prince try for her hand and a noble Venetian undertake a humiliating obligation for her, and who have heard so much verse spoken in her praise, and have been able to feast their eyes upon her for the length of three scenes, will be willing to accept her without reserve as a paragon of virtue and beauty, and the boy who undertakes the part will be incompetent indeed if he fails in it.

It is not until Bassanio comes to make his choice among the caskets [26] that Portia is shown as anything except a static figure, and in this scene she exhibits the characteristic verbosity of the Shakespearian comedy heroine, revealing her emotions through subtle and expressive poetry.   The scene reaches its climax not when Bassanio finds her portrait in the leaden casket, but when she yields herself to him in a speech of wonderful tenderness and modesty, which, in its delivery, requires to be given with artistic restraint. Here, as so often with Shakespeare's women, the psychological action is all implicit in the verse, and if this is spoken intelligently and appropriately, without too great an intrusion of the actor's personality, and with suitable accompanying physical action, the necessary effect is achieved completely, and anything of over-acting destroys the illusion.

The Trial Scene would present none of the difficulties to the boy actor that it does to the modern actress of Portia. The scene contains the climax of the play, and in performance it must be treated seriously; it has been attempted in certain productions during recent years to treat the trial as a lark, with Portia's disguise as the cream of the joke. This is an amusing presentation but it harms the balance of the play, and is patently a device to get over the difficult task of turning a woman into a credible young man, a difficulty which would disappear when Portia was played by a boy. Appearing as a young doctor of Padua, he would simply play the part as a young man, without resorting to an elaborate disguise or obtruding an unsuitable feminine quality into the scene. Portia, from her entrance, has command of the scene, which is carefully built round her, and in the speech on mercy she has a set-piece which cannot fail to move an audience. There is a tendency in modern productions of the play for the actress to attempt to make this speech an unobtrusive part of the scene, as though Portia were treating Shylock to a few observations on mercy which the other characters were not supposed to hear. It is unlikely, however, that the boy actor would forgo the opportunity to display the beauty of his elocution or the round of applause with which the speech is usually greeted.

Portia in the last act is once again female, and has exchanged the impressive robes of the Paduan doctor for her woman's garments. At her first appearance in this Act she makes a slighting reference to her voice, saying:

> He knows me as the blind man knows the cuckoo
> By the bad voice.

and it is a special charm in her, who is praised by everyone, to depreciate herself. The play closes with a long, witty passage in which she takes a leader's part.

Nerissa does much to contribute to the character of Portia and in turn basks in her reflected glory. The two are never seen apart, and Nerissa serves the office of confidante and *alter ego* to Portia. The real 'second lady' of the play is Jessica, who has her opportunity of dressing as a boy and, in a subsidiary plot, has a love affair with Lorenzo. Nothing is said of her before she appears, but her obvious unhappiness and her avowed lack of sympathy for her father, by this time labelled as the villain of the play, and in the next scene Lorenzo's praise of her [27], establish her in the affections of the audience.

A passage which is of particular interest to this discussion is the scene in which Portia reveals to Nerissa her intention of going to Venice disguised as a man. Having sent Balthasar to fetch lawyers' robes and books, she says to her confidante:

I 'll hold thee any wager,
When we are both accoutred like young men,
I 'll prove the prettier fellow of the two.
And wear my dagger with a braver grace,
And speak between the change of man and boy,
With a reed voice, and turn two mincing steps
Into a manly stride; and speak of frays
Like a fine bragging youth; and tell quaint lies
How honourable ladies sought my love,
Which I denying, they fell sick and died;
I could not do withal: then I 'll repent,
And wish, for all that, that I had not kill'd them;
And twenty of these puny lies I 'll tell,
That men shall swear I have discontinued school
Above a twelvemonth: I have within my mind
A thousand raw tricks of these bragging Jacks,
Which I will practise. [28]

It might seem that the speech in which Portia satirizes
the vanity and boastfulness of the young gallant might
take a special point from the fact that it was spoken by
a boy. Tempting as this supposition may be at a first
glance it seems unlikely that an Elizabethan audience
would find anything particularly amusing in it. To
an audience Portia is Portia and it is of little consequence whether she is a boy or a woman off the stage.
The tendency of Elizabethan dramatic technique, and
particularly in the plays of Shakespeare, is to take great
pains to present the boy actor as a woman, and not
to disturb that illusion when it has been established.
This was rendered much easier by the existence in the
minds of Elizabethan audiences of well-defined types
of the heroine, the hero, and the villain. There are
many instances in the plays of Shakespeare in which
the female characters make remarks which might be

taken as drawing attention to the fact that they were
played by boys, but this does not happen until they
have been thoroughly established in the minds of the
audience as women, and a conviction of this kind,
when once it has become a part of the play, is difficult
to disturb by a mere passing phrase or action.

MUCH ADO ABOUT NOTHING

Beatrice is generally regarded as one of the most
remarkable of Shakespeare's comedy heroines, and in
performance she shows outstanding brilliance in a
brilliant play. Her character is implicit in the plot;
she is a noble lady, Leonato's niece, and when her
cousin is wronged she wishes for revenge. Her love-
affair with Benedick is as much a witty war as their
relation before Hero and Ursula tricked her into it.
It is obvious then to anyone undertaking the part that,
if Beatrice can be made witty enough, the part will
look after itself, and as superbly witty lines are provided for her to speak, it is merely a question of actor's
technique to bring Beatrice into her proper relation to
the other characters.

At only two points has Beatrice any call to express
an emotion dissociated from her wit. One of these
is in the church, when she urges Benedick to kill
Claudio [29]. From the exit of the wedding-party the
scene is so written as to subordinate Benedick to
Beatrice, and when she has made her extraordinary
request his lines become mere interjections in an
avalanche of angry words from her. In performance

this gives her every advantage, and creates an impression of violence of emotion and strength of character without putting an unreasonable strain upon the capabilities of the boy actor. The other instance is the soliloquy in which Beatrice decides to entertain Benedick's reported love. Here she says:

> What fire is in mine ears? Can this be true?
> Stand I condemn'd for pride and scorn so much?
> Contempt, farewell, and maiden pride, adieu!
> No glory lives behind the back of such.
> And, Benedick, love on; I will requite thee,
> Taming my wild heart to thy loving hand:
> If thou dost love, my kindness shall incite thee
> To bind our loves up in a holy band;
> For others say thou dost deserve, and I
> Believe it, better than reportingly.   [30]

It is illuminating to compare these ten formal lines with the soliloquy in which Benedick admits to himself that he is in love:

This can be no trick, the conference was sadly borne; they have the truth of this from Hero. They seem to pity the lady: it seems her affections have their full bent. Love me? Why, it must be requited. I hear how I am censured, they say I will bear myself proudly, if I perceive the love to come from her; they say too that she will rather die than give any sign of affection. I did never think to marry: I must not seem proud: happy are they that hear their detractions, and can put them to mending. They say the lady is fair,—'tis a truth, I can bear them witness; and virtuous,— 'tis so, I cannot reprove it; and wise, but for loving me,—by my troth, it is no great addition to her wit, nor no great argument of her folly, for I will be horribly in love with her.— I may chance to have some odd quirks and remnants of wit broken on me, because I have railed so long against marriage: but doth not the appetite alter? A man loves the meat in his youth that he cannot endure in his age. Shall quips and sentences, and these paper bullets of the brain, awe a man from the career of his humour? No, the world must be peopled. When I said I would die a bachelor, I did not think I should live till I were married. Here comes Beatrice. By this day! she's a fair lady, I do spy some marks of love in her.

When their brief passage of wit is over, he concludes the scene thus:

Ha! 'Against my will I am sent to bid you come in to dinner'; there's a double meaning in that. 'I took no more pains for those thanks than you took pains to thank me'; that's as much as to say: 'Any pains that I take for you is as easy as thanks.' If I do not take pity of her, I am a villain, if I do not love her, I am a Jew. I will go get her picture. [31]

The actor who undertakes the part of Benedick has to make clear to the audience the complicated mental processes of a man who, although flattered to think himself loved, hesitates to fall in love himself, and yet finally does so. It will scarcely be argued that the female nature is more direct and forthright than the male, and that Beatrice's submission owes its brevity to this. It is a plain fact that Beatrice's soliloquy, brief and formal in its expression, is easily made effective by a boy actor, and that Benedick's involved heart-searchings require great skill to act them adequately. Benedick is written to be played by a comic actor of genius: Beatrice is written for a boy actor with an agreeable personality and a high degree of technical skill.

An interesting feature of this play is the intimate boudoir scene [32] in which Hero is being dressed for

her wedding. Shakespeare never again attempts
anything of this kind, and it is possible that this and
the short comedy scene which follow it were written
to allow time for the preparation of the church scene.
The scene does nothing to further the action of the
play, but it provides an excellent opportunity for Margaret, which is a comic part, as opposed to Beatrice,
which is a witty part, and is a brief scene of relief
in a play which never becomes deeply serious. It is
certain that in performance it would provide an opportunity for very skilful playing by three boy actors in
three opposed roles—Hero, the romantic heroine;
Beatrice, the witty lady of comedy; and Margaret, a
gentlewoman written as a stock comic character, an
'agreeable rattle.'

AS YOU LIKE IT

In *As You Like It* the heroine and her confidante are
again presented in an expository scene which enlists the
sympathy of the audience and presents Rosalind as an
unfortunate but richly deserving lady [33], and Celia as
a generous friend. This is followed by a passage with
Touchstone and Le Beau in which, by jesting with the
Clown and making fun of the foreigner, both are
established as witty young ladies, and when Rosalind
reveals her sudden love for the young wrestler it seems
only right that so charming a person should be so
impetuous in her decision. The convention of the
validity of love at first sight governs much of the
action of the play, and unless it is accepted without

question the romances of Oliver and Celia and the
infatuation of Phoebe with Ganymede seem improb-
able and the satire of Touchstone and Audrey merely
makes them appear more foolish.   Rosalind's expressions of love, though delicate, can scarcely be called
subtle, and her gift of the chain and her:

> Sir, you have wrestled well, and overthrown
> More than your enemies.   [34]

make it clear that she is deeply in love, and this impression, once given, remains valid throughout the play
and allows her, in the forest scenes, to concentrate
more upon the saucy lackey than upon the lovesick
maiden.

The friendship into which Orlando enters with the
supposed Ganymede would be more credible to an
Elizabethan audience than to one at the present day.
To the Elizabethans, or to the courtly class among
them, boys and women were amusing creatures with
whom somewhat flirtatious friendships for the pleasure
of witty conversation were commonplaces of daily life,
and in the case of the boys it is unnecessary to suppose
that such friendships implied any sexual irregularity.
Nowadays there are plenty of people who enter into
precisely such relationships with children, encouraging
them to become familiar for the pleasure of hearing
their quaint and clever back-answers.   In modern productions of this play the scenes in which Orlando woos
Ganymede are apt to yaw treacherously between a
supposedly masculine roughness and heartiness and
moments of sticky feminine sentimentality.   Actresses
are rarely able to make Ganymede boyish without

assuming a coarse and hectoring mien which is entirely
out of key with the part and leaves the audience the
impression, when he says:

. . . an old religious uncle of mine taught me to speak,
who was in his youth an inland man, one that knew court-
ship too well . . .

that his old religious uncle must have been an impostor
who never saw the inside of a court. Similarly, in
their more coming-on moments, few actresses are able
to resist the temptation to be coy, which is merely
vulgar and something which no lady of Rosalind's
breeding would stoop to. Now a well-trained and
clever boy, guided in his performance by a poet, would
be able to strike just the right note of high-comedy
and to play the part of Rosalind disguised with delicacy, because he would not feel it necessary to over-
stress any aspect of his character; when, at last, he
resumed his woman's clothes, he would resume his
woman's manners with them.

In this play, as in *Much Ado About Nothing*, the witty
heroine is given the advantage over all the other
characters greatly to her own aggrandizement. Even
Jaques, who has no difficulty in crushing every one
else, is quite put down by Rosalind [35].

Upon the whole, Rosalind is a part admirably suited
to the capacity of a boy actor of more than ordinary
skill. There is what might appear to be a difficult
moment when Rosalind, hearing of Orlando's encounter with the lioness, swoons, but upon examination the difficulty disappears. The intense emotion
which overcomes her when she hears of her lover's

danger is expressed by a few minutes of silence, during which Oliver completes his story, and then she swoons, an easy but effective device to show deep feeling which she shares with Hero and, though in a very different situation, with Lady Macbeth.

The elaborate basis of stage convention upon which the play is built is further illustrated near the conclusion, where the duke, who does not recognize his daughter, says:

> I do remember in this shepherd boy
> Some lively touches of my daughter's favour.

and receives a reply which shows that Orlando has not recognized the girl whom, nevertheless, he loves. In a world where such things can happen any slight artificiality in the boy Rosalind would escape unnoticed. Celia presents no difficulties in performance, and Phoebe is given charm and individuality by the delightful verse which she speaks; as a part to act, hers cannot compare for a moment with that of the ill-used Silvius in difficulty.

The Epilogue of *As You Like It* is exceedingly interesting, as having been spoken by a boy, a fact which points to extraordinary ability on his part, and gives rise to some speculation as to what the effect of such an epilogue would be. Rosalind is a part which would demand, in the boy who played it, not only a fine command of technique, but a pleasing person and that indefinite quality of charm which, in the theatre, is as potent in men as in women. The boy who advanced from among the other players to speak this speech would be invested not only with the distinction

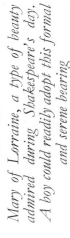

Mary of Lorraine, a type of beauty admired during Shakespeare's day. A boy could readily adopt this formal and serene bearing

Nell Gwyn, whose great popularity was chiefly due to the exploitation of her beauty and natural talent for bu

of an actor who had played his part well (and we may
assume that if he were entrusted with a leading part he
would be able to play it to his employers' satisfaction),
but with the charm of Rosalind herself, which would
create in him a glamour equal to that of some of our
modern actresses. To judge by the speech itself, he
exercised his charm upon the men and women of the
audience alike, and in his double character of clever
and pretty boy and clever and pretty girl he would be
of great interest to both, and in a very personal way.
Common observation in daily life shows that few
women can resist the charm of a handsome boy,
particularly if they believe him to be innocent, and in
this way the boy Rosalind would appeal to the women
whom he charges to like the play; men are notoriously
indulgent toward pretty girls, and in this form the boy
appeared to the men in the audience, emphasizing his
femininity by his:

. . . I charge you, O men, for the love you bear to
women,—as I perceive by your simpering, none of you
hates them——

Then notice the cunning of the conclusion:

If I were a woman, I would kiss as many of you as had
beards that pleas'd me, complexions that lik'd me, and
breaths that I defied not: and, I am sure, as many as have
good beards, or good faces, or sweet breaths, will, for my
kind offer, when I make curtsy, bid me farewell.

It is a common assumption that all of this is addressed to the men in the audience, but from what has
gone before it need not be accepted as true. The
beards are a male prerogative, but good complexions

F

e the property of either sex, and in Elizabethan
ngland a stinking breath was usually considered a
womanly fault, from the eating of sweetmeats. Therefore Rosalind may well have offered to kiss men and
women alike, and all present, for no one would be
likely to think his beard a poor growth or her breath
disagreeable. The stipulation, 'if I were a woman'
would save the offer from giving offence to the
strait-laced, without robbing it of any of its pro-
spective delight. The art with which this epilogue
exploits the appeal of the boy actor to both women and
men in the two parts of his professional personality
is remarkable. In the modern theatre the much-
discussed quality of 'sex-appeal' can only be made to
work upon one sex at a time; the boy actor could, and
in this epilogue did, appeal to both sexes at once,
which is more than the most widely advertised of our
modern 'World's Sweethearts' can hope to do.

TWELFTH NIGHT

As there seem to be good grounds for assuming that
the boy who played Rosalind was an unusually good
actor, and as *Twelfth Night* is the next play to appear in
the canon, it is possible that he played Viola as well,
for the part is a logical advance from Rosalind, being
considerably more difficult to play, for a variety of
reasons. First, Viola is not a witty heroine; true, she is
far from being a dullard, but her prevailing temper, her
humour, is not witty. Secondly, she moves through
the play alone, and is the first of the comedy heroines

(for even Katharine has a meek foil in Bianca) to appear without any sign of the obliging confidante or cousin who acts as her *alter ego* through the play. This is a more serious deprivation than it might at first seem, for when two people appear on the stage together as Portia and Nerissa, or Julia and Lucetta, or even Beatrice and Hero, scenes of exposition, or scenes in which secrets are confided, are possible, and character can be established in a simple and easy manner. This isolation of Viola gives added effect and pathos to her character as a young girl attempting to endure a hard fortune which is denied to Rosalind. It marks also an advance in Shakespeare's technique as a playwright, that he can draw so complete a character as Viola without resort to the time-worn device of the con-✗ fidante, for the only intimate allowed her is the Sea Captain, and when she leaves him she is alone in the play and must depend on acting ability rather than convenient dialogue to keep her place of importance in a cast containing several attractive comic characters, who might easily assume first place in the estimation of the audience.

Another reason for believing that Viola was played by the boy who played Rosalind is that, although Viola says at her first appearance:

> . . . I can sing,
> And speak to him in many kinds of music,
> That will allow me very worth his service,

she never does sing, and the songs in the play are given to the Clown. A boy with sufficient experience and intelligence to play Rosalind might be fifteen or sixteen ✗

years old, and by the time he was called upon to play
Viola, at seventeen, he would be less sure of his
singing voice than would be desirable. There has
been much discussion as to whether the songs in the
play were transferred from Viola's part to that of
the Clown, and this suggestion concerning the age
of the boy actor affords one reasonable excuse for such
a change, although it is unlikely that the question will
ever be settled definitely.

An interesting passage is that in which the Duke
praises the femininity of Cesario's appearance, saying:

> For they shall yet belie thy happy years,
> That say thou art a man: Diana's lip
> Is not more smooth, and rubious; thy small pipe
> Is as the maiden's organ, shrill, and sound,
> And all is semblative a woman's part.   [36]

The effect of this speech would be to remind the
audience that the page was a woman disguised, and in
a few more lines Viola confesses that she herself loves
the Duke, in a brief soliloquy, with a directness which
is characteristic of these confessions on the part of
comedy heroines.   In the scene which follows this [37]
Viola and Olivia speak in prose as long as they are
engaged in bantering, but as soon as Viola begins her
praise of Olivia's beauty she speaks in verse, and the
effect of this change is to give a sudden lyric lift to
the whole scene which is of striking dramatic value.
Although Olivia replies in prose, she soon falls under
the messenger's spell and speaks in verse herself, and
the whole effect of this mechanical device is to raise the
scene to a higher plane, which is of great assistance to

the actors. In this part of the play soliloquies are used lavishly, for Olivia confesses her love for Cesario in one, and later when Viola guesses that Olivia loves her she confides her bewilderment to the audience in another [38].

Viola's love for the Duke, owing to the nature of the plot, must be concealed and given indirect expression only, and the scene in which this is brought about [39] contains some of the finest poetry in the play. It would be stupid to overlook the effect of the song, 'Come away Death,' in establishing an atmosphere of romantic melancholy, and this is a fact which can only be appreciated by watching the play in performance. The air, first played and later sung by Feste, hangs over the scene and colours it through and through with its peculiar sweet sadness and its implication of unrequited love. It would not be ridiculous to suppose that the song was introduced to help Viola in her delivery of some of her loveliest lines, for the song is undoubtedly meant to establish an atmosphere, and the atmosphere is of the greatest value to her, and the beauty of this scene, in which she tells of her love while the Duke is concerned only with his hopeless suit to Olivia, does much to win the affection of the audience at an early stage in the play.

The part of Sebastian is not particularly interesting, as it seems designed for an actor of no more than ordinary ability, who is cast as the twin of the principal boy of the company. He has some fine verse to speak, and his soliloquy before he goes to marry Olivia [40] is the sort of long expository speech to which a boy actor

would be accustomed, and which he would no doubt
recite with full appreciation of its poetic quality. The
encounter of the twins in the last Act is managed
skilfully; the emotion appropriate to the reunion
is represented adequately in the verse, and only a
minimum of action is possible.

Another interesting part for a boy actor in this play
is that of Maria. It requires an unusual charming
vivacity which can be maintained without monotony,
and a talent for infectious laughter. As Maria's diminutive stature is mentioned several times the boy would
necessarily be small, and probably younger by two or
three years than the actors of Olivia and Viola. Small
women are common in Shakespeare's comedies, and
Leonato's short daughter, and Hermia and Maria, may
have been written for boys who were noticeably small
even when allowance was made for the ordinary
difference in height between men and women.

THE MERRY WIVES OF WINDSOR

There is little subtlety of characterization in the
women's parts in *The Merry Wives of Windsor*, for
rapidity of the action and the broad nature of the
comedy makes it unnecessary. The roles of Mrs Ford
and Mrs Page may very well have been played by
youths of any age between seventeen and twenty, for
small boys would seem ridiculous on the stage with
Falstaff, and the parts have an authority and a forth-
rightness which is not typical of the boy actor parts in
the other comedies. It is certain that Mrs Page was

considerably taller than Falstaff's page Robin, for she
calls him 'eyas-musket' and 'little Jack-a-Lent' [41].
There is no need for the wives to be either dainty or
very beautiful, for they are not romantic but comic
figures, and in so robust a play as this the extra three
years between fifteen and eighteen would give the
necessary breadth of style and yet leave the boy with
a serviceable voice and all his talent for female
impersonation.

The discovery of the imposture which has left
Slender and Dr Caius each with a great lubberly
boy [42] would perhaps be more amusing to an
Elizabethan audience, which was accustomed to boy
actors, than it is to an audience to-day. To mistake a
clown for a beautiful boy actor would be funnier than
to mistake him for a beautiful actress, because as both
were boys, the disparity was not of kind, but of
quality, and consequently the joke had a subtlety
which must be lost to-day. However, this is a very
slight matter. The boy who played Anne Page, by
the way, may easily have been more beautiful than
talented, for she has little enough to do, and takes no
part in Fenton's defence of their elopement.

ALL 's WELL THAT ENDS WELL

The useful device of the soliloquy is employed again
by the heroine of *All 's Well that Ends Well* to confess
her love for Bertram of Rossillion [43], and later in the
same scene she expresses in another soliloquy [44] a
point of view which may be taken as a justification of

her subsequent somewhat jesuitical conduct. Helena
is little more than a puppet in a dramatized 'tale,' and
her actions are dictated by the exigencies of the plot;
the first soliloquy conveniently clarifies her position
as a maiden deeply in love, and the second makes it
plain that she regards any means as fair which will help
her to win her beloved. She has still another soliloquy
which is presumably meant to awaken the pity of the
audience for her, and, if it were delivered skilfully it
might do so, for in this play, in which no character
rises to any great height of nobility, and in which the
hero cuts a very poor figure, even allowing him the
grace of the convention under which anything that
the hero does is right, the heroine may claim whatever
sympathy the spectators have to spare. It is certain,
however, that the pleasure of seeing this play must lie
almost entirely in the unfolding of the plot, and the
characters make very little direct appeal to the audience.
Helena's trickery and her sententious repetition of the
ambiguous maxim which gives the play its name are
not engaging characteristics, but the part has enough
vitality to carry it through the play with considerable
success. The lack of subtlety in the writing, however, would beget a corresponding directness in the
acting, and the part is an easy one from a technical
point of view.

MEASURE FOR MEASURE

In *Measure for Measure* the part of Juliet is not
important to the play, but it provides an interesting

example of the mingled conventionality and realism of Elizabethan acting. She appears with Claudio [45] as the evidence of his guilt, but says nothing, and seems to have been brought on the stage only to give point to his words to Lucio:

> But it chances
> The stealth of our most mutual entertainment
> With character too gross is writ on Juliet.
> *Lucio.* With child, perhaps?
> *Claudio.*   Unhappily, even so.

From this very direct reference to her plight in the dialogue it may be assumed that she bore some visible mark of pregnancy, perhaps the cushion to which Doll Tearsheet had recourse [46], and this sort of realism, practised by a boy actor, would be unlikely to give offence. When actresses came to the stage dramatists agreed to forgo effects of this sort, and pregnancy, as a device to excite pity, almost disappeared from the stage until the coming of the problem-play in the nineteenth century, and, probably owing to a feeling of delicacy on the part of the actresses, the cushion convention has not been revived.

Measure for Measure, like *All 's Well that Ends Well*, is primarily a play of situation, and to play it effectively it would be necessary to subordinate interest of character to interest of plot. This is made difficult by the extraordinary fullness with which the part of Angelo is drawn, so that it is always a temptation to an actor of first-rate ability to play it as a study of character. If he does so, however, the rest of the company, attempting to follow his example, upset the balance of the play

by trying to put more into it than it can conveniently
hold, and all the weakness and ugliness of the dramatized 'tale' are exposed. The part of the heroine,
particularly, suffers by too close an examination of
her motives. Isabella is a straightforward picture of a
woman possessed by what, for the purpose of dramatic
expediency, the audience agree to regard as a high
ideal from which she will not depart, until the plot
demands that she do so. Whatever there is of subtlety
in the conflict between Isabella and Angelo is expressed
in his part, as in the two soliloquies in which he is
shown struggling between lust and duty [47]. Throughout the scene of Isabella's attempted seduction the
actor of Angelo is required to express a conflict
between inclination and discretion, and to reveal his
purpose slowly, until he is driven by her coldness to
a display of cruelty. Throughout the scene Isabella
is never once required to change from her pose of
rectitude. The scene is a subtle piece of stagecraft
and Isabella has much the best of it on the moral side
(for a maiden resisting seduction may always count on
the whole-hearted support of the audience), but no
great strain is put on the actor's technical ability, for
Isabella has only one pose here and elsewhere in the
play. But as Katharine seems to partake of Petruchio's violence, so Isabella seems to an audience to
be concerned in Angelo's struggle, and the better he
acts it, the more her part gains thereby. Audiences
do not, and should not, discriminate while watching
a scene, between the actor who is acting, and the actor
who is being acted *at*, if the expression is permissible,

and in many of Shakespeare's most impressive scenes
an approach from an actor's point of view will reveal
that one character is active, and the other passive.   It
does not follow, of course, that because the former
must be a fine actor the latter may be an incompetent drudge, but it is true that the passive part
is easier to play because it makes less demand on
the emotional resources, and it is possible to make
such parts extremely effective without too much
difficulty.   In Shakespeare's plays the heavy burden
is always cast upon a part which would be played
by an actor of experience and power, and generally
therefore upon a man.

In the prison scene [48], in which Claudio suggests
to his sister that she should accept Angelo's bargain,
her steadfastness is contrasted with his fears and his
weakness and again the burden of the acting is cast
upon the man, for to give adequate expression to
Claudio's despondency and dread of death is considerably more difficult than to stand by and speak
noble words.   Isabella's outburst of vituperation [49]
may seem, in reading the play, to show a hardness of
heart which is unlovely in a heroine and a nun; in
performance the danger of the audience receiving such
an impression would be negligible, for the speech,
though bitter, would be spoken by a beautiful woman
in the very becoming costume of a Poor Clare, and it
would be taken as a defence of her virginity.   The
reflection upon the virtue of her mother was a common-
place of Elizabethan thought, and the violence of her
speech in rejecting what the audience regard as an

infamous proposal would rather commend her to their affection than displace her from it. An audience would have no opportunity to exercise that critical faculty which is responsible for so much comment on the plays and to them Isabella's dictum:

More than our brother is our chastity   [50]

would be as valid as it is to her. An audience rarely rejects a play in part, and if it accepted Isabella at all, as it very probably would, it would accept her rigid code of morality as well.

Nobility of character is considerably easier for a well-graced actor to portray than depravity, for nobility is usually passive in poetic drama; it is the norm, and whatever falls short of it must justify itself by being exceptionally interesting. So Isabella presents no difficulties to the boy actor, though Angelo is a part in which an actor of remarkable qualities might fail, so complex is it, even when no determinedly 'psychological' approach is adopted. All good acting should be psychological but there is rarely any need for it to become psychopathic, and perhaps Shakespearian actors would play better if they forgot the very little psychology which they have read and concentrated upon the text.

THE WINTER'S TALE *and* THE TEMPEST

The nobility of Hermione is simple to act (if the actor knows what nobility is, which frequently he does not), and creates a profound impression in performance, whereas the violence of Leontes, even when he is given the benefit of the stage convention which makes slander easily credible and suspicion a law unto itself, is surprisingly sudden and theatrical in the worst sense of that word. It is interesting to notice in a performance of this play how much the character of Hermione gains by her appearance as a 'living statue' in the concluding scene. This device seems to change her from the stock wronged wife into a goddess who, having been restored to her husband by these remarkable means, brings all of her marmoreal purity with her.

Neither Perdita nor Miranda presents any difficulties as parts for boys. Both are required to be pretty, charming, and capable of speaking fine verse well, and these are qualities which any boy actor of the first rank would have readily at his command. They are entirely straightforward and need no detailed examination.

There are, in the comedies, several women's parts which cannot be classed as heroines or confidantes, but which do not differ so markedly from the ordinary run of boys' parts as to require discussion in Chapter IV, and these may be mentioned briefly here. The first of these is Luce, in *The Comedy of Errors*. She makes a brief appearance 'above' [51] and has a few lines of back-chat with Dromio of Ephesus and it is unlikely that in a performance of the play she would attract any particular attention. Still, she is the first of Shakespeare's comic women and, as such, deserving of mention. It is a matter for genuine regret that the kitchen-wench, Dowsabell, does not appear on the stage. Dromio of Syracuse gives an elaborate description of her [52], and she is mentioned by him several times [53] with a relish that gives her a greater reality than any of the women who are concerned directly in the action of the play.

Jaquenetta, the beloved of Don Adriano de Armado, is a laconic and dull-witted young woman who, paradoxically, is funniest when she is off the stage; her first interchange with the fantastical Spaniard is brief and diverting [54], but she seems much more amusing when Adriano's letter to her is read by Boyet [55] and the audience are permitted to contrast what they hear said of her with what they have seen.

Jaquenetta is hardly a part of first-rate importance, and may have been doubled with that of Mercade, as both of them could be played by a young man. Audrey, in *As You Like It*, however, is a prominent part, and considerably more demanding than Jaquenetta, which might be regarded as a preliminary study for it. In the Elizabethan theatre Audrey was probably played rather more broadly than is usual in modern performances, and her foulness would leave very little to the imagination, but the part does not lend itself readily to downright clownishness; Audrey has many really good lines to say and a sensible actor would not spoil his chance of making his performance genuinely funny by introducing more comic business than the part would conveniently hold. It seems likely that both Jaquenetta and Audrey were played by half-grown youths, who had passed the boy actor stage, but whose experience would fit them admirably for the comic female roles.

Mopsa and Dorcas in *The Winter's Tale* are rustic maidens, but there is no reason to suppose that they were played as low-comedy parts. Their lines are amusing, but they are never required to be very funny, and it is unlikely that in their scene with the Clown they would be allowed to be so. Their song in the same scene is sufficient proof that the parts would be filled by boys whose voices and appearances would allow them to play the ordinary run of women's parts.

It is interesting to notice that in three of Shakespeare's comedies, *Much Ado About Nothing*, *As You Like It*, and *Twelfth Night*, the parts of heroine and 'second lady' are given to a tall boy and a short one. Beatrice, Rosalind, and Viola are all parts which demand not only a distinguished presence and a very certain and brilliant technique but also a warmth of personality and a charm which suggests that they were written for one player. The parts show a natural progress from Beatrice, who is witty but not very much else, to Rosalind, who is witty, but in a deeper and more human way, and here and there tinged with melancholy. Viola has the melancholy developed to a greater degree, is not witty except incidentally but, because of her secret despairing love for the Duke, is invested with a depth which is not found in the other two.

Mr M. R. Ridley, editor of *The New Temple Shakespeare*, suggests as well a relation of Helena and Hermia and Portia and Jessica to Rosalind and Celia and Olivia and Viola, and has omitted the pair from *Much Ado About Nothing* altogether. Accepting the dates most favourable to such a supposition, and placing *A Midsummer Night's Dream* in 1598 and *Twelfth Night* in 1602, it is quite possible that a pair of boys of first-rate ability may have played the principal parts in all five plays, and parts can be found for them in the plays which intervene.   It has been suggested in this chapter that the player of Viola may have reached an age where his voice was no longer trustworthy for singing, and there can be no doubt that a boy of seventeen or eighteen would play Viola better than one who was still a child; it would be easier to find a suitable twin for him in a company in which boys were less numerous than men.   Supposition of this kind is dangerous, for the seeker after relationships between one Shakespearian character and another may be betrayed by his enthusiasm into extravagances of improbability; nevertheless, it seems reasonable to suppose that the chief women's parts in these five comedies were played by the same boys, for the parts, both those of heroine and 'second lady,' increase in difficulty in a surprisingly logical fashion and may parallel the increased technical skill and the gradual rounding-out of personality of two unusually gifted boy actors.

This picture of *Queen Elizabeth by an unknown artist gives
some idea of the guise in which Cleopatra appeared to
Shakespeare's audiences. The management of such a costume
demands a queenly bearing*

CHAPTER III

The Women's Roles in Shakespeare's Histories and Tragedies
discussed with reference to the Boy Actor

In Shakespeare's historical plays there are very few parts for boy actors and these are rarely of first-rate importance. The obvious reason for this is that in wars and troublesome reigns women usually play an unobtrusive part if they are concerned in them at all, and the Elizabethan dramatist, with his all-male cast, was under no pressure to distort historical fact in order to provide a meaty part for a leading actress or a film star whose principal talent lay in the lifelike depiction of glamorous courtesans. It is necessary, also, to remember that the historical plays had a topical interest for Elizabethan audiences which is considerably weakened to-day, and the rancour of the Wars of the Roses and the struggle for power between the king and the cardinal were matters which might at any time become dangerous realities in the life of the nation. The writing of the histories is vigorous and full-blooded, and they lend themselves to violent and impassioned acting. It would be wrong to say that they are more violent than the tragedies, but it is true that the violence of the histories is external whereas that of the tragedies is inward, and represents the struggle of the soul. The histories would have a particular appeal to that part of the audience which delighted in pageantry and the resounding delivery of rhetorical speeches, and the plays are written with sufficient of both these elements to ensure their popularity. The fights and battles which are such a problem to the modern producer were then one of the most satisfying parts of the entertainment and although the Prologue to *Henry V* has been quoted as proof that the representations of battles on the stage were inadequate it may easily have been written in that spirit of modesty which merely enhances what is to follow. Self-depreciation has at no time been a characteristic of theatrical advertisement, and it is extremely unlikely that Shakespeare would have mentioned the limitations of his stage if he were not confident that the performance would exceed the expectations of his audience. But there is little in these plays of tenderness, or of relief from the highly rhetorical style of delivery and action, and in such an atmosphere the boy actor must necessarily take a very inferior place, as he could not hope to compete in violence and noise with the actors of kings and warriors. The historical play was the Elizabethan actor's opportunity to roar and to rant, and it is likely that he did it very well, and it is certain that the presence on the stage of skilled swordsmen must have made the battle-scenes exciting and dangerous. In displays of this sort the audience did not want to see boy actors, and their roles are usually those of weeping queens or bashful princesses who provide some slight relief from the stress of the main action and introduce a pleasantly romantic note into the spectacle.

THE THREE PARTS OF KING HENRY VI

The scenes of *Henry VI, Part I* in which Joan la Pucelle appears are considered by many critics, and notably by Sir Edmund Chambers in his *William Shakespeare* (vol. i, pp. 282–93), not to have been written by Shakespeare. As the play is included in the canon, however, it can do no harm to touch upon the character here.

Joan la Pucelle is regarded by many critics as a repellent character, and receives very little consideration from them, and the part is certainly not an amiable one. In performance, however, it would undoubtedly stand out with a kind of coarse strength, and that curious attractiveness which always surrounds a truly abandoned woman, particularly when she is also a beauty. Valiance and fighting ability were much appreciated in women who were not presented to the audience as ladies of gentle birth, and Joan was probably as popular with the audience as Moll Frith a decade later, when she delighted the town in Thomas Middleton's play, *The Roaring Girl*, in 1611. It is a matter of opinion whether the spectacle of a woman brawling on the stage is an entertaining one, and the squeamish must be permitted to have their say. Elizabethan audiences liked lively performances and there is no question that Joan is very much alive and that her depravity has an unusual fascination about it.

The coarseness of Joan's character is of a kind which a woman would find difficult to express adequately, but which a youth could manage with ease. Particularly is this so in the scene of Joan's martyrdom [1], when she begs for clemency on the ground that she is with child.   The scene is in no way 'written down' in order to make it possible for the boy playing Joan to achieve his success by delicacies of technique.   The lines must be shouted, and the repudiation of the old father must be done with a violence of scorn possible only to a few actresses.   It is interesting also to notice the coarseness with which Joan proclaims her pregnancy and the gleeful fashion in which York and Warwick discuss the possible fathers of the child.   It is futile to discount this scene as an example of Elizabethan boorishness; the scene has the ring of truth, but it is a truth that modern audiences do not care to recognize, nor would a modern audience be comfortable at a representation of this play in which an actress was called upon to speak so indelicately, and two actors were required to mock at her for having been gotten with child.   The situation is one which must always be objectionable to some spectators, but it cannot be denied that it is splendidly effective drama, which is what the Elizabethans wanted, and what they got. Although they were capable of relishing scenes such as this, which our weaker stomachs reject, they inspired their poets to flights which ours cannot equal. We have paid for our humanitarianism by a narrowing of our emotional field, and our theatres are noisy with the jingle of teacups.

Queen Margaret is a character which was probably played by a boy past the first boy actor or heroine period, who would be able to manage the vigorous

lines which are given to the part, without being
hopelessly lost among the warriors who crowd the stage.
Her first speech [2] is preceded by a complimentary
reference from the king, which is followed by yet
another, and the general acclaim of the kneeling
courtiers helps to establish Margaret as an important
character. Her quarrel with the Duchess of Gloucester [3] is written without subtlety, and the exchange
between the two women, though brief, must be played
with sufficient strength to give it the importance which
it needs in the play. Margaret's complaint at the
King's excessive grief for Gloucester is expressed in
a long passage of formal verse [4], and in her subsequent
farewell to Suffolk her grief is shown by technical
means which are sufficient for the purpose and lessen
the demand upon the actor for a display of deep
emotion. Such tricks are the kissing of his hand [5],
and the go-and-do-not-go structure of the speech,
which has a curious power to suggest grief in parting,
perhaps because it gives expression to an emotion
which is often felt but, except on the stage, very rarely
expressed. Even in the scene in which she embraces
Suffolk's head [6] her emotion is of a formal kind, and
it is likely that to an Elizabethan audience, to whom
severed heads were commonplaces in the drama, frequently serving as poignant reminders of the dead
lover, as in the tale of *Isabella and the Pot of Basil* in the
Decameron (Nov. 5, giorn. iv), this would not seem
unusual.

Margaret's first entrance in the third part of the play
is well prepared by the dread of Exeter and the King,

and their fear of her anger establishes it even before she speaks; throughout this part of the trilogy she is the 'wrangling woman' [7] of Edward's reproach, and at last the 'captive scold' [8] of Gloucester's. York's long and abusive speech [9] does much to impress Margaret's character upon the audience, and works up an atmosphere of violence before she stabs him which makes the act doubly significant; it may be noticed that York's reference to her as an 'Amazonian trull' [10] indicates that the actor of Margaret must have been of some stature, and gives support to the supposition that it was played by an older, and consequently taller boy than was usual.

The wooing of Lady Grey [11] by King Edward is badly written and its lack of nuance is accentuated by the stichomythia in which much of it is cast. The scene perhaps is introduced for relief, and to help in elucidating the character of Gloucester. In any case, Lady Grey is a very minor role, easily filled by a boy of no great talent.

RICHARD III

The most interesting scene in *Richard III* from the point of view of this discussion is that in which Richard woos Lady Anne [12]. The scene opens with a grieving speech, cast in the familiar formal mould, in which Lady Anne mourns for King Henry, and by her appearance in the garb of a widow, and by her professions, establishes herself in the minds of the spectators as a bereaved and heart-broken woman. After the brief commotion which follows Gloucester's appearance, he says:

Sweet saint, for charity, be not so curst,

to which she replies:

Foul devil, for God's sake hence, and trouble us not,

and after a further burst of grief, which once more recalls her forlorn condition, they enter on a dialogue consisting of antithetical speeches, fairly evenly matched in length, and in each speech of Gloucester's he advances his cause a step farther; as he does so, her replies, which are all in the same vein, seem less and less effective. The formality of the dialogue is here used to suggest the hypnotic fascination of Richard by his gradually encroaching replies, in each of which he turns her words into a potent charm. The formal nature of the dialogue permits a more direct approach than a naturalistic method could do, and paradoxically the formality of the scene, and the convention of the boy actor which is a part and cause of the formality, gives a greater illusion of credibility than could be achieved in any other way, and gives this eerie wooing the elaborate pattern and beauty of a dance, and a poetic reality far above mere naturalism. The preliminary speeches finished, Richard enchants her into submission in a long speech [13], and eventually wins her by the theatrical trick of putting his life in her hands. She yields, and is won in a few short, pregnant lines [14], and when Anne departs she is Richard's. Throughout the scene he bears the full burden of the action, makes every advance and every suggestion, and after Lady Anne's exit he explains away any lingering doubts the audience may have in a soliloquy [15]. The part of Lady Anne is simplicity itself both technically and emotionally; she is entirely passive, and her part derives all its effect from Richard.

Throughout the play Queen Elizabeth and Lady Anne are not called on for any very decisive action and their scenes seem static in comparison with the rest of the play. The keynote of the Queen's character is grief, and this is shared by Lady Anne when she has become Richard's queen. Elizabeth has one speech of remarkable pathetic quality [16], which gives life to her character. Otherwise she makes no great demands on the actor, and it may be that the women's parts in this play reflect the mediocrity of the boys available to play them.

It is interesting to notice the parallel between Richard's wooing of Lady Anne and his wooing of Queen Elizabeth for the hand of her daughter [17]. The same tricks of antithesis and stichomythia are used and an odd effect is given of echoing the earlier courting. In this too the woman is the passive, and Richard the active figure, bearing the acting burden of the scene.

RICHARD II

The part of the Queen in *Richard II* is of very little importance, and for this reason, in notable modern productions of the play, when actresses of first-rate importance are cast for the part, several devices are used to give the Queen an importance which is not

warranted by the text. Thus in the two most important
revivals in recent years the Queen was introduced into
the scene in the lists as an ornamental figure; and in the
scene of Gaunt's death, where she has only one line of
greeting to the old man and then presumably waits in
the background for the King, she was made to leave
the stage with a show of deep concern at the news of
Gaunt's death, accompanied by Northumberland, to   ✗
return in time for her exit at the end of the scene.   It
was remarkable to what a degree these comings and
goings increased the value of the part, and without
some such padding no actress of the first rank would
be likely to undertake it.   As it stands in the text,
however, the part is a poor one, and its true function
seems to be to excite sympathy for Richard, and his   ✗
Queen is no more than one facet of a many-sided
character.   Thus her forebodings and her formal and
conceited expressions of grief at his downfall [18] are
not so much important in revealing anything of herself as they are in impressing upon the spectators the
essentially personal side of Richard's tragedy, as opposed to the kingly side of it, and this is shown clearly   ✗
in his outburst in Act V, Scene 1:

> Doubly divorced! Bad men, you violate
> A twofold marriage, 'twixt my crown and me,
> And then betwixt me and my married wife.

The Queen has little purpose other than to be decorative, and to suggest a side of Richard's character not
otherwise touched on in the play.

Another piece of business with which modern producers have sought to build up the part of the Queen

is this: when she is parted from Richard in Act V, Scene I, she kisses his hand during the concluding lines.   In Act V, Scene v the Groom, upon entering, kisses Richard's hand, and he, remembering his Queen, holds it to his lips with a strong show of emotion. This device, though it has no warrant in the text, is deeply moving in performance; it is indicative, however, of the extent to which Shakespearian production is influenced by fashion, for the public at present will have a 'love-interest,' by hook or crook, in every play. These tricks also gloss over the allegation of homosexuality which Bolingbroke makes against Richard [19], which is distasteful to a modern audience, and alienates their sympathy from the hero.

HENRY IV, PARTS I AND II, *and* HENRY VIII

The women's parts in *Henry IV* are likewise of very minor importance, with the exception of the comic characters, who are discussed in Chapter IV.   Lady Percy is brisk and outspoken even in her grief [20], and her first scene with her husband is designed more to reveal his character than hers.   Lady Mortimer's part is interesting as having been written for a boy who could both sing and speak Welsh [21], and therefore probably a Welsh boy.   This part may well have been played by Robert Goffe, who was a member of the Lord Chamberlain's company.   His name is a common one in Wales, being derived from *gôf*, a smith.

The role of Queen Anne Bullen in *Henry VIII* is principally ornamental, and would require an actor of exceptional physical beauty and grace, in order to mark the contrast between Anne and the ageing and sickening Queen Katharine. Her first appearance is at Wolsey's banquet [22] where she has only three brief speeches, but she is important in the action as she is chosen as the King's partner and is presumably engaged in considerable by-play with him. Next she is seen in a scene with an Old Lady which shows her sympathy with her unfortunate mistress and displays in her a naïve and trusting nature which is oddly at variance with historical fact but which would appeal * strongly to an audience who knew her as the mother of a great queen who was but ten years dead. Her final appearance is in her coronation procession. Anne requires beauty and charm, and acting ability is a very secondary consideration in casting the part.

The women of the histories are of no very great interest, as they are in most cases mere puppets. Now and again they flash into life through a few lines of fine verse which is given them, but in the main they are unimportant in a type of play which was written to provide parts for the Ned Alleyns of the Elizabethan stage. The women of Shakespeare's tragedies, how-ever, are an entirely different matter, and must be discussed at some length.

TITUS ANDRONICUS

Titus Andronicus is the tragedy of a family, the chief representative of which is Titus himself, and the char-acters of his four sons and his brother Marcus and his

daughter Lavinia have very little reality considered
apart from him. The relation between Titus and
Lavinia is strong dramatically, as the relation between
parent and child usually is on the stage, and considered
from the point of view of the producer, the character
of Lavinia is as closely bound up with that of Titus as
Cordelia's is with Lear, and, as in the later tragedy, the
daughter exhibits an aspect of the protagonist which at
first seems foreign to him, and in turn the character of
the daughter gains dramatic strength and significance
from this close relation to the protagonist.

Lavinia is first introduced into the play when
Bassianus speaks of her as:

Gracious Lavinia, Rome's rich ornament,   [23]

and so awakes in an Elizabethan audience a host of
associations with the romantic Rome of their imagina-
tions and the traditional nobility and virtue of its
women, and soon Lavinia herself appears to do rever-
ence to the memory of her slaughtered brothers,
expressing herself in formal terms which establish her
as the type of Roman maidenhood, pious and chaste,
an impression which deepens during the whole of
this Act. This opinion is increased by the description
given of her by Demetrius and Chiron when they
quarrel about her [24], and when, at Aaron's prompt-
ing, they plot to ravish her. The effect of a scene of
this sort on an audience must not be overlooked, for
although the reports of Lavinia's chastity would be
sufficient to convince them of its reality, a plot to rob
her of it would impress it upon them as nothing else

could, and her chastity, from being one attribute of her character, would become her character itself, and the loss of it would be a minor tragedy. A curious expression of Lavinia's indifference to carnal pleasure is contained in her reproof to Saturninus when he suggests that the hunt has been begun too early [25], and this would provide an unfavourable comparison between herself and the abandoned Tamora, which is strengthened by Lavinia's speech in the following scene, in which she exercises the privilege of virtue to rebuke vice and does so with marked asperity [26]; it will be noticed that this is her first positive speech in the play. Later in the same scene, when Chiron and Demetrius are about to carry her away to ravish her, there are frequent references in the text to her womanhood [27], and although these may be considered inevitable in the circumstances, the repetition of the word 'woman' seems almost to be intended to force Lavinia's sex upon the attention of the audience by auditory as well as by visual means, to increase the excitement of the scene and to augment the horror of her approaching rape.

The nobility and chastity which have been attributed to Lavinia thus early in the play make her next appearance [28] even more painful and shocking than it would be ordinarily. The direction is:

Enter Demetrius and Chiron with Lavinia, her hands cut off, and her tongue cut out, and ravished.

Her mutilations are symbolic of her ravishment and are outward and visible horrors, intended to shock and disgust the spectators; if they heard of Lavinia's rape in the dialogue and she appeared before them distressed but not visibly inconvenienced her misfortune would lose its tragic proportions. The loss of hands and tongue do not need very subtle interpretation to be shown as symbols of a hideous rape, and as Lavinia and Titus are, for dramatic purposes, one, the outrage is not only an offence against his daughter but a serious blow aimed at himself. Throughout the remainder of the play the loss of Lavinia's hands and tongue are constant reminders of the ruined fortunes and declining powers of the Andronici.

The repellent nature of Lavinia's rape and her subsequent physical appearance in the play have effectually barred it from the modern stage, but there is reason to suppose that it was popular in its day. No modern audience would care to see a woman brought before them, horribly mutilated, to be mocked at by her ravishers [29], and the scene in which she fumbles the books with her stumps [30] would revolt some spectators, and drive others to that laughter with which shallow minds greet what is pathetic without being noble. The convention of the boy actor provides a solution to the problem, for his impersonal and formal method of acting would make Lavinia's anguish [31] less real and, without lessening their dramatic effect, would provide a reassurance that her mutilations were merely a part of the play [32]. Unfortunately, however, to modern audiences the suffering in this play does not seem to bring about the tragic catharsis which would excuse it, and consequently it appears merely as a brutal and savage story. The psychological implications of its wealth of mutilation and horror are too disquieting to be endured when it is acted with any degree of realism.

The heroine's role is written to place as little strain as is possible in such a part upon the actor of Lavinia. When she is discovered by Marcus his grief, expressed at length, reflects hers [33], and it is unlikely that she would do more than stand in an attitude of despair while he spoke. So also, in her meeting with Titus, Lavinia's grief is confined to a very little dumb-show [34], and the burden of the acting falls upon him. From this point onward Lavinia is merely a reminder of the woes of Titus, until the ghastly scene in which she assists at the murder of Chiron and Demetrius. Such a character as Lavinia is only possible in a highly artificial play, in which the acting is largely formal and externalized. Too great an attempt at realism in the performance of this part would upset the balance of the play.

The character of Tamora is likewise artificial, but consistent within a very limited emotional range. At her first appearance [35] she mentions her tears, but it is unlikely that she had very much opportunity to weep in the course of her seventeen-line speech, as the habit of the Elizabethan stage was rapid utterance, with few pauses except for important by-play. Aaron's long speech in praise of her [36] is valuable in establishing her character as an adulteress and a wanton, and so gives weight to the one passionate scene between them [37]. The whole problem of the extent to which physical love-making was shown on the stage during the time of the boy actor will be dealt with in detail in

Chapter V, but it is necessary here to point out that some physical expression of passion is inevitable in this scene, and Aaron cannot refuse Tamora's advances until she has made them. Such a passage as:

Tam. Ah, my sweet Moor, sweeter to me than life!
Aar. No more, great empress; Bassianus comes: [38]

must, in the context, imply some effort on her part to embrace him, or draw him to her, and however conventionally this is done its significance remains unmistakable. The formal show of physical passion was a part of the boy actor's equipment which he was frequently called upon to use. Tamora is a simple character, and the naïveté of her lines:

Ne'er let my heart know merry cheer indeed
Till all the Andronici be made away.
Now will I hence to seek my lovely Moor
And let my spleenful sons this trull deflower, [39]

marks her out for very obvious playing, as only by such means could this and her appearance as Revenge [40] be given any sort of credibility. The actor who undertook Tamora would play with gusto, and there would be no question of his attempting to make the character lifelike.

JULIUS CAESAR

The type of the noble Roman lady occurs again in Portia, wife of Marcus Brutus. The part is interesting, for it leaves an impression on the spectator of beauty and fidelity, but much of this impression is given by Brutus's tender solicitude for his wife in her first scene [41]. Her next appearance serves to work up an atmosphere of excitement for the approaching catastrophe. The part is a trifling one, and would be discharged with ease by any competent boy actor.

Calpurnia, also, is an unimportant character, introduced once [42] to give point to one unimportant speech of Caesar's [43], which illustrates a picturesque incident drawn from Plutarch. Her later appearance [44] is more interesting and here she serves as a foil to Caesar to show his pride and courage by contrast. The character, as such, scarcely exists, but in its undistinguished form it throws the strength of Caesar into relief.

Mr Harley Granville-Barker, in his *Prefaces to Shakespeare* (First Series), has written about Portia and Calpurnia with great insight and feeling, and has enlarged upon their characters as far as is possible. The fact remains that they are of very slight importance to the play and, in a company where there were no actresses to be cajoled into thinking that they had important roles, the parts were obviously meant to give the usual relief, and to aid in the adherence to the tale of Caesar's fall as told in Plutarch; many of their speeches are paraphrases of North's translation of 1595.

KING JOHN *and* TIMON OF ATHENS

On more than one occasion Shakespeare introduces into his tragedies women who have little justification other than that they are decorative, and so provide a

H

useful relief. Such characters are Blanche of Spain in
King John, and Phrynia and Timandra in *Timon of
Athens*, who appear only to lend point to Timon's
violent outburst against women. They are mere stage
furniture, used to illustrate a sort of meretricious
character which will submit to any abuse in return for
gold. The chief requisite for these parts is beauty.

PERICLES

Another role which has very little importance except
as decoration is that of the daughter of Antiochus in
Pericles, Prince of Tyre; both her father and Pericles
speak at length of her beauty [45] but her one speech
is an unimportant couplet, introduced perhaps to keep
the part from being completely dumb. Antiochus's
daughter would seem more important in performance
than she does in an examination of the text of the play,
for she had all the qualities of a fairy-tale princess, and
it is a principle of stagecraft that a character who is
unimportant to the plot of the play gains greatly by
standing perfectly still and silent on the stage while the
other characters act around and at him.

Marina in *Pericles* is another Shakespearian tragedy
heroine who suffers an attempt upon her virtue, but in
this case she is successful in defeating it. It can hardly
be maintained that Marina is a lively or frivolous girl,
and her first speech strikes rather an unsympathetic
note of self-pity, but the line:

This world to me is like a lasting storm,   [46]

gives the key to her character as one doomed to misfortune. The long speech with which Gower has
ushered in the fourth Act has impressed upon the
audience that Marina is a paragon of accomplishment
and virtue, and has awakened the envy of her foster-
mother, and before her appearance her character has
been built up to the point where the action can begin
with her attempted murder; Marina takes the attempt
upon her life calmly, on the whole, and her show of
fear finds its expression in a well-reasoned defence,
probably performed in some formal position of plead-
ing, as kneeling with the hands clasped. In her next
appearance in the bawdy-house at Mytilene, Marina is
given the advantage which comes to the actor who is
allowed to stand still for a time without speaking, and
the impression she made would be the result rather of
the pity of the audience for a maiden in her position
than of any pantomime on the part of the actor.
Marina says little at any time in this scene, but, as she
is the centre of interest in it, that little has great weight
and would be certain to have a deep effect on the
audience. The climax of the scene is her declaration:

> If fires be hot, knives sharp, or waters deep,
> Untied I still my virgin knot will keep.
> Diana, aid my purpose!   [47]

and in this one speech the boy actor reaps the benefit
of the atmosphere which Boult and the Bawd have
built up throughout the scene. The situation is the
common stage one by which the character who opposes
the general tone of a scene is thrown into strong relief
and given an apparent strength by so doing.

It would be careless, also, to underestimate the
dramatic value of the contrast between Gower's speech
before Marina's monument [48], with its highly effective inscription, and the second brothel scene which
directly follows it. Pandar, Bawd, and Boult again
work up an atmosphere of depravity, while also describing and making more credible Marina's stout
resistance to the attempts which they have provoked
upon her virginity. The subsequent passage between
Marina and Lysimachus is reminiscent of the attempted
seduction of Isabella by Angelo [49], for here again the
chief acting burden falls upon the man as seducer,
while the sympathy of the audience is with the woman,
whose task of depicting innocence and passive resistance is a comparatively easy one. Her chance to make
a deep impression comes in her speeches to Boult [50]
when she rebukes him for his ignoble profession and
urges him to help her to escape. Her success in her
new task of teacher is again described by Gower in his
prologue to the fifth Act, and the meeting of Pericles
and his daughter is so arranged that the joy of recogni-
tion is expressed by him in speech, and the easier task
is again allotted to the boy actor.

The scenes in the brothel which are usually supposed
to be so disfiguring a feature of this play would nevertheless, moralistic consideration apart, act exceedingly
well, for the Pandar, Bawd, and Boult part of the
dialogue establishes a remarkable atmosphere of de-
gradation and ethical obliquity above which Marina,
by the trick of construction already considered,
triumphs completely, and the wretchedness of their

souls enhances the purity of hers.   Again it may be
repeated that in the Elizabethan drama virtue is the
norm, and the characters who depart from it must
exert themselves to portray evil; the virtuous character,
as with Marina, is static, and profits by their labours.

TROILUS AND CRESSIDA

In *Troilus and Cressida* the boy actor who undertook
the part of Cressida was required to present the
character of a shallow and faithless woman, which
would at first seem to make a very heavy demand upon
him, but a careful examination of the play shows that
this is not so, and reveals that the technical devices
which have been employed formerly to invest the
woman's role with charm and depth of character are
here employed with equal success to show her in an
exactly contrary light.   In this play, perhaps more than
any other, the effect of the principal woman's part
depends upon the success of the hero, for as the actor
of Troilus is able to show disillusion and grief, so will
Cressida seem false and meretricious.   Because of this
close sympathy, it is almost impossible to consider the
roles separately, and in the subsequent discussion
Troilus will be compared with Cressida in order to
show the difficulties of the one part and the means used
to put the other within the boy actor's capacity.

Troilus opens the play, in itself a difficult task for
a principal character, for the first few minutes of a
performance must be used to gain the full attention,
not merely the silence, of the spectators, and to set the

tone and pace from which all the rest of the play will
proceed. When this task falls upon the hero it
increases his burden considerably, for not only must
he establish his character as hero, but he must do the
hard work of the first five minutes, and pave the way
for all that is to come.   In this first scene Troilus is
shown in an agony of love for Cressida, and if he does
it well her character gains so much thereby, and the
great outburst of passion beginning [51]:

> O Pandarus!   I tell thee Pandarus—
> When I do tell thee there my hopes lie drown'd,
> Reply not in how many fathoms deep
> They lie indrenched,

does as much to fix Cressida's beauty and desirability
in the minds of his hearers as it does to convince them
of his own passion.   The scene presents many technical difficulties, not the least of which is the presence
of Pandarus, for although the contrast between the
worldly old scoundrel and the poetic lover is characteristic of the play, it does not diminish the difficulty
of building up romantic climaxes where there is no
support from the other actor on the stage, and particularly so when this is a man of first-rate quality
playing an excellent part.

Cressida's first appearance [52], on the contrary, is in
a straightforward comedy scene, presenting no difficulties of execution, but giving plenty of time for
Cressida to impress herself upon the audience, and in
her soliloquy [53] she reveals the withholding and
flirtatious quality of her nature.   In a heroine of
tragedy such astute calculation is not an engaging

quality, and this speech, in performance, has the effect
of alienating the audience from Cressida, and their
subsequent attitude towards her is one of mistrust.

When Troilus and Cressida first meet [54] the man is
given again the more demanding role, for he has to
show a violent emotion imperfectly held in check, a
more difficult matter than a straightforward show of
passion. The actual difficulties of the moment of
meeting are considerably alleviated by Pandarus's
comic commentary, but when he leaves the lovers
alone, Troilus's speeches are sincere and passionate,
and those of Cressida evasive and somewhat bantering
and her eventual declaration of love coy and in-
sincere [55]; the lovers formally declare their love
and faith in two speeches of almost equal length [56],
and the forehand knowledge of Cressida's character
gives this scene a strong ironic flavour.

When next they meet Troilus is infatuated and
Cressida peevish and disagreeably coy when she says:

My lord, come you again into my chamber.
You smile and mock me, as if I meant naughtily.
Tro. Ha, ha!
Cre. Come, you are deceiv'd I think of no such thing. [57]

Her hysterical outburst when she learns that she must
leave Troy is useful, as it is full of vigorously pro-
tested faith to Troilus which in performance is
strikingly ironic, as it is now clear to the audience
that Troilus is deeply in love and Cressida is not, an
impression which is made even more definite in the
scene of their final parting [58]. Here again Troilus
is given the difficult task of expressing sincere grief

amid Cressida's wailings and Pandarus's foolish
babblings; the impression of instability in her nature
is increased by her wounded protests when Troilus
urges her to be true, which, although they must be
said sincerely, in the circumstances are only another
proof of her fickleness, for by this time even an
audience unacquainted with the story must be fully
conscious of the difference between the lovers. At
such a time lines like:

O heavens! you love me not!

are sure marks of shallowness, on the stage at least.

The whole question of physical love-making in
Shakespeare's plays will be discussed in Chapter V,
but at this point it may be interesting to notice the part
which it takes in this play. The first kiss of the lovers
is 'a kiss in fee-farm' [59], apparently a prolonged and
passionate embrace, and there is another shortly afterwards [60]. There is yet another [61], which is the
occasion of a display of coyness on Cressida's part,
making up the number to three kisses, obviously
passionate, prominently set in the action. Later there
is a positive orgy of kissing in the Trojan camp [62],
when Cressida is kissed by Agamemnon, Nestor,
Achilles, and Patroclus; it cannot be argued that these
were mere greeting-kisses, as the accompanying dialogue reveals more than a merely courteous interest on
the part of the generals, and the jokes on the subject
with Menelaus and Ulysses show that the kisses were
regarded as gallant attentions; these kisses make a
striking contrast with those of Troilus, and Cressida's

gratified acceptance of them, even from the dotard Nestor, is meant as a clear sign of her promiscuous nature, a point which Ulysses thrusts home with considerable force when he says:

> Fie, fie upon her!
> There 's language in her eye, her cheek, her lips,
> Nay, her foot speaks, her wanton spirits look out
> At every joint and motive of her body.
> O, these encounterers, so glib of tongue,
> That give a coasting welcome e'er it comes,
> And wide unclasp the tables of their thoughts
> To every ticklish reader!   Set them down
> For sluttish spoils of opportunity,
> And daughters of the game.   [63]

The first definite knowledge the audience receives of Cressida's treachery is contained in a soliloquy of Thersites [64], a source which gives it a peculiarly disagreeable quality, utterly removing any possibility that there can be an excuse for her conduct.   In the scene immediately following, Troilus is an eavesdropper to a passage between Cressida and Diomedes which also contains a certain amount of physical intimacy, as is shown by Troilus's:

> She strokes his cheek!

and that this is not an isolated action, but rather a part of a fairly elaborate by-play is suggested by Thersites's comment:

> How the devil luxury, with his fat rump and potato finger tickles these together!   Fry, lechery, fry!

In the business with the sleeve objective action reflects the supposed psychological action of the characters, and

Cressida's giving it, and taking and then yielding it again are more indicative of her flirtatious and vacillating nature than if she gave it outright, which would seem a simple transfer of her love from Troilus to Diomedes.   The last that is seen of Cressida is when she speaks her brief soliloquy at the end of this scene [65], which is an apology, perhaps, for her behaviour though the audience would be likely to endorse Thersites's terse comment on it.   Throughout the play Cressida has been shown as a foolish and shallow girl, and every appearance and speech of hers is designed to further this end.   The part presents no difficulties because of its remarkable consistency; in this play, where shallowness and foolishness are the norm, Cressida is no worse than the rest.   The spirit of the play is bitter and disillusioned, and Troilus has the task of showing romantic trustfulness and innocence in this uncongenial atmosphere.   This is a neglected play, for it is too salty for the public taste, but it must always be a favourite with those who delight in irony, and who are not repelled by its vivid representation of a disagreeable but very common aspect of human nature.

The other women in the play are of minor importance.   Cassandra has perhaps the most surprisingly dramatic entrance of any woman in Shakespeare [66], for she bursts upon the Trojan commander with only the briefest indication from Troilus of who she is. There would be no attempt on the Elizabethan stage to give a subtle rendering of Cassandra's prophecies. Her speech presents several purely elocutionary difficulties which the boy actor would be trained to meet more than adequately, and the part, in performance, gives valuable relief in a scene which tends towards dullness.

Helen is a simple comedy part, and the chief necessity in the actor of it is beauty; in Shakespeare's day this would mean the fair English beauty of Elizabeth, with the distinction and grace which her Welsh and Italian blood gave her. It is an amazing tribute to the ability of the boy actors to suggest grace and beauty that both Shakespeare and Marlowe provided them with opportunities to appear as Helen of Troy, the Renaissance ideal of beauty, and that there is no contemporary suggestion that they were not equal to the task.

CYMBELINE

The part of Imogen, in *Cymbeline*, has fidelity as its ruling characteristic; it is upon this quality that the plot revolves. Imogen resembles Rosalind and Viola in the peculiar problems presented to the boy actor who undertook the part. He would necessarily have a mastery of the technique of acting used on the Elizabethan stage, and in addition an unusual charm of personality, which would enable him to carry a part upon which the chief interest of the play is centred. Imogen would tax the powers of such a one, but the part is written with allowance for the limitations of the boy actor and is given every aid of stagecraft.

An initial advantage is given to the part of Imogen in that it contains no conflict, but presents its chief quality of fidelity to the audience so consistently that its effect is cumulative. Of the three principal roles, Posthumus, Iachimo, and Imogen, she is the only one who is unchanging, for her husband, from being devoted to her, changes until he doubts her virtue, and then realizes his error and begs her forgiveness; and the villain repents his evil ways. This consistency of Imogen's makes the part easy to act emotionally, for no change of attitude is necessary, and the role is really a series of variations on a single theme.

A characteristic of Imogen which is not noticeable in the other heroines of tragedy is her gift for brief, poignant speech. To quote examples seems needless, as this quality has been remarked upon by many critics of the play and must impress even the casual reader, but it can do no harm, and may help to make clear the dramatic advantage which such speeches give. An excellent example comes when first Posthumus leaves her and Imogen says:

> There cannot be a pinch in death
> More sharp than this is, [67]

and yet another when Iachimo tells her of her absent husband's faithlessness:

> My lord, I fear,
> Has forgot Britain. [68]

These speeches give a vivid impression of sharp suffering held in check which contributes immeasurably to the nobility of Imogen's character. An example of another kind comes when Pisanio, commanded to murder his mistress, says:

> O gracious lady
> Since I receiv'd command to do this business
> I have not slept one wink.

and Imogen replies:

> Do 't, and to bed then. [69]

showing a bitterness which can only excite pity.
Imogen has, for a Shakespearian heroine, the unusual
trait of seeming to feel more than she says, a condition
which is not easy to show on the stage. These
moments of deep feeling, however, are scattered
through the play, and are magical in their immediate
effect, so that, without laying upon the actor the
necessity of playing a scene of any length in which
repressed emotion is the dominant note, there are still
sufficient of them to give a remarkable cumulative
effect, and the technique of the boy actor and his own
emotional resources would be sufficient to carry him
over these difficult moments triumphantly.

Like Rosalind, Imogen has the advantage of wearing
boy's dress during a very important part of the play,
which would allow the boy actor to depend more upon
his own personal charm than upon his skill as a female
impersonator; it would allow him to exercise to the
full the talent for pathos which is characteristic of all
sensitive adolescents and which can be turned to the
very best dramatic account. The frailness of his
physique, also, would be instrumental in arousing the
pity of the spectators, and this frailness would be
enhanced by his appearance in doublet and hose when
previously he had been seen in the bulky and majestic
costume of a court lady. When first Imogen comes

on the stage in boy's costume [70] she has a soliloquy,
which would enable the audience to accustom themselves to the change, and there is a very noticeable
increase in the pathos of this speech over Imogen's
part in the preceding action, and this pathos is clearly
marked in the soliloquy which she speaks when waking
to find the headless body of the supposed Posthumus
by her [71].   This speech presents elocutionary difficulties, but the boy who played it could set his own
pace and tone and work out the necessary variations
within the limits of his own resources.   It must be
stressed that in this difficult soliloquy the boy is not
hampered by the presence of another actor on the stage
against whom he must measure his strength; the
effectiveness of his acting depends on the skilful use
of his own vocal equipment and pantomime on an
empty stage, and if he has any real acting ability, this
is a heaven-sent opportunity to show it at its best.

Before leaving the consideration of Imogen it will
be well to notice that in the scene in which Iachimo
tries to seduce her [72] he very noticeably takes the
active part and she the passive one.   It may be argued
that the situation makes this relation inevitable, but
there are several scenes in modern drama which are
similar in theme, in which the woman takes the active
role at least part of the time.   Comparisons between
modern and Elizabethan drama can never be wholly
satisfactory as their technique and convention are so
dissimilar, but as an instance of a scene of seduction in
which the woman, instead of being the innocent and
passive agent, is at times the aggressor, the second Act

of Maeterlinck's *Monna Vanna* is interesting, and the
second Act of G. B. Shaw's *The Apple Cart* and the
whole of Ferenc Molnar's *The Guardsman* illustrate a
technique of handling scenes, roughly of this sort, in
which the burden of the action is equally distributed.
In this particular scene, however, the great part of the
acting burden falls on Iachimo, and Imogen is given
only one speech which contributes to the building up
of the atmosphere:

> Away! I do condemn mine ears, that have
> So long attended thee. If thou wert honourable
> Thou wouldst have told this tale for virtue, not
> For such an end as thou seek'st; as base as strange,
> Thou wrong'st a gentleman who is as far
> From thy report as thou from honour; and
> Solicit'st here a lady that disdains
> Thee and the devil alike. What ho, Pisanio!
> The king my father shall be made acquainted
> Of thy assault: if he shall think it fit
> A saucy stranger in his court to mart
> As in a Romish stew, and to expound
> His beastly mind to us, he hath a court
> He little cares for, and a daughter who
> He not respects at all.

This is straightforward denunciation, requiring no
subtlety in its delivery. In scenes of this kind Shakespeare places the burden where it can best be borne, and
as the actor succeeds in his task, so the boy actor who
does his best with the easier role allotted to him benefits
by the atmosphere which is established.

ROMEO AND JULIET

Shakespeare is rarely at pains to give the ages of his heroines, but in the case of Juliet it is made clear at her first appearance that she is not yet fourteen. There would be nothing remarkable about this fact if it were not that in the sources of the play she is described as being older. In *Romeus and Julieit* by Arthur Broke (1562) this line appears:

Scarce saw she yet full xvi yeres: too young to be a bride.

and in *Rhomeo and Julietta*, published in Painter's *Palace of Pleasure*, in vol. ii of the quarto of 1567, the following passage gives her age:

. . . the Lord Antonio willingly agreed, saying unto her: 'Wife I have many times thought upon that whereof you speak, notwithstanding sith as yet she is not attained to the age of .xviii. yeares . . .'

Shakespeare's definite statement that Juliet is not yet fourteen seems to point to the fact that the boy who played the part was either very young or of small stature. The writing of the part produces some evidence in support of the first supposition, for although it makes heavy demands on the actor technically, it does not ask that extra quality which Rosalind, Viola, and Imogen all require; it does not need their charm. Juliet demands enthusiasm above everything, and equipped with this and with a fine technique, particularly of elocution, a boy would not find the part unduly difficult. There is, of course, a saying current in the theatre and among some critics, that an actress does not know how to play Juliet until

she is too old to look the part.   This is one notion of
Juliet, born perhaps of a reverent but unintelligent
approach to Shakespeare; there is no question that the
injection of mature passion into the role does it great
harm.   Juliet demands a display of youthful passion,
a quality which very few young actresses seem able to
express adequately, and in their hands she becomes a
bread-and-butter miss, filled with treacly yearnings;
this conception of the part is as bad as the matronly
one, substituting, as it does, a foolish schoolgirl for the
brilliant and burning heroine of Shakespeare's creation.

In this play, as in *Troilus and Cressida*, it is significant
that of the male and female protagonist, the heavier
acting burden falls on the former.   Romeo, when first
he appears, is in love with Rosaline and this fact is
well impressed upon his audience; later in the play he
falls in love with Juliet, and the actor is faced with the
task of showing the difference between these two
passions, with the difficulty that, if he makes the first
too shallow, the second may appear to be shallow also,
and he will appear merely as a person of fickle affections.   The scene with Friar Laurence [73] helps him
in this to some extent, but the difficulty is still present.
Compare, for instance, his outburst in praise of
Rosaline:·

> She 'll not be hit
> With Cupid's arrow; she hath Dian's wit
> And in strong proof of chastity well arm'd
> From love's weak childish bow she lives unharm'd.
> She will not stay the siege of loving terms
> Nor bide the encounter of assailing eyes,
> Nor ope her lap to saint-seducing gold:

I

O, she is rich in beauty, only poor
That, when she dies, with beauty dies her store.

with that when he first sees Juliet:

O, she doth teach the torches to burn bright!
It seems she hangs upon the cheek of night
Like a rich jewel in an Ethiop's ear;
Beauty too rich for use, for earth too dear!
So shines a snow-white swan trooping with crows,
As this fair lady o'er her fellows shows.
The measure done, I'll watch her place of stand,
And, touching hers, make blessed my rude hand.
Did my heart love till now? forswear it, sight!
I never saw true beauty till this night.

The difficulty of differentiating these two speeches
without scamping the first is considerable.

The first meeting of the lovers is cast in the formality
of a sonnet, which is admirably suited to the boy actor's
art, and which has the effect of isolating the lover's
speeches from the rest of the scene.   In the celebrated
balcony scene the expression is poetic but not formal
and it is primarily in poetry, rather than in action, that
Juliet declares her love.   It could be argued that Juliet
is given much the best of this scene and that her
speeches are superior to Romeo's; such cheeseparing
distinctions seem out of place in the consideration of
a scene of such beauty, but it is a fact, merely from the
point of view of stagecraft, that Juliet has the advantage of being on the balcony, or upper stage, and so
would attract more attention than Romeo, who is on
the ordinary level.   The result of this disposal of the
characters is to give extra value to everything that
Juliet says.

The actor of Romeo has another difficult problem to
face in the scene in which he refuses to fight with
Tybalt, for here he must show first a strong emotion
kept in check, and after the death of Mercutio a
conflict of violent feeling within himself [74] which
changes to anger. The actor's task here is to show
the change from one emotion to another clearly, but
without obvious and mechanical means. It is interesting to compare this scene with that which follows it,
which begins with Juliet's brilliant bravura:

> Gallop apace, you fiery-footed steeds
> Towards Phoebus' lodging:

a magnificent opportunity for a fine speaker to give an
impression of overwhelming passion by purely elocutionary means. Here Juliet has the stage to herself,
always a great advantage, and can adjust the delivery
of the speech to suit her capabilities, without the
danger of any more robust actor provoking a comparison, and the soliloquy would appear to the
audience as an isolated display, rather than as an
integral part of the scene which follows it. In this
scene her first change of emotion is to grief, and this is
given a formal expression in the punning 'I' and 'Ay'
speech, and her next change to a conflict of emotion is
shown in the antithetical 'Beautiful tyrant! fiend
angelical' speech, which again gives a formal guise to
the violence of the feeling expressed. Her final outburst is in the long speech in which the word
'banished' rings in the ears and again produces an
effect of grief and despair by a mechanical means.
Throughout this scene the actor's technique is placed

under a heavy strain, but the emotion needed in the
speeches is largely evoked by the devices which have
been shown, which, combined with the slight but
sincere emotional resources of the boy actor, would
give a thoroughly satisfactory effect in performance.   It
is interesting to notice that Romeo's expressions of grief
in the succeeding scene have no such artificial form.

The scene in which the lovers part for the last time
shows two good examples of the formality with which
many of Juliet's emotional speeches are written.   The
first of these is that which follows Romeo's last
speech [75] in which she plays upon the words 'fickle'
and 'fortune,' with alliterative effect, and the second is
in the passage with her mother [76] where Juliet
speaks in riddles, revealing the conflict in her mind by
the ambiguities of her speech.

Throughout the play Juliet has passages of remarkably direct speech, in which her emotions are set forth
with a violence which leaves nothing to the imagination.   Her outburst when Friar Laurence suggests to
her a way of avoiding a marriage with Paris [77] is
an excellent example of this characteristic of the part.
The bravura speeches, too, are used more by Juliet
than by any other Shakespearian heroine.   The scene
in which she takes the potion is perhaps the most
valuable of these theatrically, and the long sentences
which, in delivery, are cumulative in effect, build up a
remarkable atmosphere, which is abruptly broken off
when she falls upon the bed.   This scene cannot fail
if it is performed with any skill, and once again Juliet
has the stage to herself for her difficult technical

display, and the value of this isolation in her hardest ⸲
scenes cannot be over-emphasized.

The difference between Romeo and Juliet as parts to
act lies chiefly in this fact that Juliet is written directly,
and without sudden changes from one emotion to
another, except where these are greatly assisted by the
writing of the lines.   Juliet has nothing to compare in ⸲
difficulty with Romeo's scene in which he receives the
news of her death [78]. Here he enters full of hope, only
to hear the worst possible news, which he greets with:

> Is it even so? Then I defy you, stars!

There is no long speech here in which he can pour out
his feelings; there is a brief, poignant moment:

> Well, Juliet, I will lie with thee to-night,

and afterwards his grief and his bitterness must all be
suggested indirectly in his speeches to the Apothecary.
The difference between the parts does not show
strikingly in performance, and it is not meant to do so,
but it is the difference between a part which requires
some moments of highly emotional acting, where
nothing else will do, and a part where technique and
enthusiasm can be relied upon to cover the actor's
emotional deficiencies.

HAMLET

The part of Gertrude in *Hamlet*, although it is
important in the fable of the play, presents no great
difficulties in performance. The scene in which she
appears with the greatest degree of dramatic interest is

that in her closet [79], and an examination of this scene
❦ shows that here she does very little and says very little,
but is acted upon by Hamlet.   Her part is merely to
make the speeches which provoke his replies, and to do
nothing to distract the attention of the spectators from
him, but here, as always in scenes of this character, the
Queen derives from Hamlet, and the better he acts, the
better she seems to act.   Such a part would not be
entrusted to a stupid or incompetent actor, but the
qualities which it demands are easily within the scope
of a well-trained boy.   The Queen has two fine
poetical speeches; the first is her description of
Ophelia's drowning [80] and the second is her speech
at Ophelia's grave [81].   Her death is rapid, and she is
given no chance to make a very great to-do about it,
primarily, of course, because this would hold up the
action at a crucial moment, but also because Shakespeare never trusts a boy actor with a death-scene.
Gertrude is a very good part for a boy actor, and it
has no complexities.

Ophelia also is a very simple part.   In her first
scene [82] she is quiet and modestly attentive until her
sensible rebuke to the priggish Laertes [83], and her subsequent scene with her father is perfectly simple.   In
the Nunnery Scene, as it is often called, she is merely
a foil to Hamlet, as the Queen is in the Closet Scene,
but she has her opportunity in a soliloquy [84] to
establish her character as a slighted maiden.

In the Play Scene there are a few lines [85] between
Hamlet and Ophelia which are frequently cut when the
play is performed, as it is thought that their coarseness

is a disagreeable blot on the play. Their purpose is
not difficult to discover; Hamlet is feigning madness,
and lewdness of speech is a common result of mental
illness. The lines spoken to Ophelia are meant as an
indication of his madness, and perhaps the fact that
they are embarrassing to her gives him a perverse
pleasure in his bitterness and excitement. The
presence of the boy actor as Ophelia would take much
of the offence from the incident, which is considered
disagreeable by some modern playgoers, who do not
dissociate Ophelia from the young lady who plays
the part.

Ophelia's most effective scene is that in which she
appears mad [86], and here Shakespeare uses music to
create atmosphere with remarkable effect. The boy
who played Ophelia would be a trained singer, without
doubt, and so the varying moods of the songs which
she sings would be strongly marked and would make
their proper effect upon the audience. The stage-
direction for her entrance in the First Quarto reads:
'*Enter Ofelia playing on a lute and her haire downe singing*';
the flowing hair was a conventional Elizabethan sign
of madness, and the presence of the lute means that
Ophelia, like any Court lady, is a musician and will
play and sing like one. It has already been remarked
that this is Ophelia's great scene, the scene that makes
the part worth playing, and it has become a sort of
graduation piece for actresses, as has the sleep-walking
scene in *Macbeth*. It is astonishing, therefore, that the
part is frequently undertaken by actresses who have
neither voice nor musicianship; sometimes the songs

are crooned or sung in a small and pathetic voice in order to accentuate the pitifulness of the situation. Pathetic the scene is, but it is also terrible, and this aspect of it can only be brought out by an intelligent actress who can sing.

It is unnecessary to invent tunes for these songs, for they can all be found in E. W. Naylor's *Shakespeare and Music* (1931) and were chosen for their particular effect in this scene. Shakespeare's passion for music and his fine taste in it need not be stressed here. Ophelia's first song is a love-song, with a haunting sad air in the minor, the second is a bawdy rollicking song which so gently bred a lady would not be expected to know. The contrast is both terrible and pathetic, and shows the repulsive inconsequence and untimely mirth of insanity. The coarseness of the second song is also characteristic of madness; actresses or producers who cut it because they think it unseemly or harmful to the gentle character of Ophelia show lack of insight. Many people reveal an astonishing knowledge of obscene language and of songs when their wits leave them. If this song is sung loudly and shamelessly the effect is shocking to the audience, and the interjection of 'He answers' into the second verse increases this effect as it stresses the brutality of the song and gives a disquieting glimpse of the fancies concerning herself which occupy Ophelia's moithered brain.

When next Ophelia appears she sings snatches of a sad song and soon afterwards what seems to be part of a spinning song, very different in character, and after

her play with the flowers she breaks into the old song
of *Bonnie Sweet Robin*, only to change to:

And will a' not come again?

a song which begins slowly in the minor, only to
quicken in tempo and to change abruptly to major at:

No, no, he is dead,

the most unsuitable part of the song; no better air
could have been chosen to accompany madness.

Throughout this scene Ophelia has the stage as
much to herself as if she were alone on it, and the other
actors are merely foils for her.   The art with which the
scene is constructed is staggering, and its effect in
performance is to put Ophelia among the principal
characters of the play, a position to which her other
scenes do not entitle her.   Here her songs and her
disconnected speech all centre round the loss of her
father and of her lover, strangely confused in her
unhinged mind.   The brilliant use of the songs gives
an unexpected turn to what might have been a conventional mad-scene, and by using one of his peculiar
qualifications turns it into an astonishing piece of
bravura for the boy actor.

OTHELLO

Of the women's parts in *Othello* neither Bianca nor
Emilia is difficult.   The former needs more beauty
than acting ability, and is a role of minor importance.
Emilia is not prominent in the first half of the play,
but she becomes so as the action wears on, and she has

a fine scene with Othello after the murder of Desdemona [87]; the vigour with which the part is written
and the way in which she is pitted against Othello
suggest strongly that the part was meant to be played
by a young man who had passed the boy actor stage,
but who was still effective in parts of this sort, where
his strength was an asset.

Desdemona first appears before the Senate, where she
makes a decisive speech which might appear to mark
her as a positive and vigorous character; actually it
merely serves to show and accentuate her devotion to
Othello, which is her dominant characteristic in the
play.

In her next appearance, at the seaport in Cyprus,
Desdemona plays a prominent part in a scene of light
banter, and has an opportunity to impress herself upon
the spectators as a gay and beautiful lady. The
frivolity of tone which characterizes the scene makes it
easy for Desdemona to shine in it, and to show in
herself these usual qualities of a heroine.

When Desdemona pleads with her husband to
reinstate Cassio as his lieutenant [88] the excitement
is largely held over from a previous scene [89] where
Iago has been seen plotting this very situation. As
far as Desdemona knows, all is well, and she must act
the scene accordingly, and continue so when, at her
second entrance, she loses the handkerchief. In the
subsequent scene in which Othello upbraids her for
the loss of the handkerchief she is a passive figure,
allowing herself to be hectored by her husband with
only the mildest protests, and in the succeeding scenes

she has only amazement and denials. Even when Othello strikes her she says little, and such defence as she does make is addressed not to Othello but to Iago [90].

After the passages of storm and stress, the quiet interlude which is the last before Desdemona's death comes as a welcome relief, and here, as in the case of Ophelia, Shakespeare uses the ability of the boy actor to sing in order to heighten the tragic effect and to establish an atmosphere of pathos. This similarity causes some speculation as to whether Ophelia and Desdemona were played by the same boy, for only two or three years elapse between the plays, and the parts have other similarities. No satisfactory conclusion can be reached, however, without definite evidence, and the ability to sing would be the rule rather than the exception among boy actors.

The air chosen is a particularly felicitous one, written in the minor, and with a refrain which rises for a moment into the major, only to sink again with a curious sweet melancholy. It is astonishingly effective in the atmosphere which it evokes, and it adds immeasurably to the beauty of Desdemona's character. There are several modernized versions of this air, which misrepresent it, and some later settings of the words which are not satisfactory. It is common in modern productions for Desdemona to sing the song without accompaniment, and this is very rarely successful; in the Elizabethan theatre there can be little doubt that the song was accompanied by a lute or viols or a combination of both. An excellent transcription of the original air and accompaniment is printed in volume one of *English Ayres, Elizabethan and Jacobean*, edited by the late Peter Warlock and Philip Wilson, and the breaks in the vocal part are obviously the pauses during which Desdemona's interjected requests to Emilia are spoken.

The scene of Desdemona's murder does not call for any great effort from her. Here again she derives from Othello, and her pleadings seem pitiful in proportion as his passion is violent and destroying. The burden rests wholly upon him and Desdemona can add nothing to the scene by attempting to share it. Professor A. C. Bradley, in his essay on *Othello* in *Shakespearean Tragedy*, says of Desdemona:

If her part were acted by an artist equal to Salvini and with Salvini for Othello, I doubt if the spectacle of the last two Acts would not be pronounced intolerable.

This is surely a misapprehension; the sort of acting needed for Desdemona is quite different from that which is suitable to Othello, and any attempt on her part to rival him in his own field and to steal the play would ruin the effect of the tragedy. An actress who was Salvini's equal as an artist would know the limitations of Desdemona too well to attempt to eclipse the tragic protagonist. The strength of Desdemona is her weakness, which is stressed throughout the play. A curious and effective stroke of stagecraft, which gives a peculiar beauty to the role of Desdemona, is that by which Emilia, in dying, repeats a phrase of the Willow Song, thus reminding the spectators of the pathos of her death.

KING LEAR

The three daughters of Lear are of unusual interest in the discussion of the boy actor, for two of them are quite outside the ordinary range of women's parts and the third, the heroine of the tragedy, appears seldom and says remarkably little, but nevertheless seems to bulk very large in the impression which an audience receives of the play. This may be explained in part on the ground that Cordelia is the only passive character in the tragedy; all her misfortunes are undeserved, and yet her nature remains unchanged, and in a play in which the usual standards of virtue are violently outraged, she remains pure and faithful. Though passive, Cordelia is not weak; the drawing of the character is simple in outline, and the actor who undertakes it cannot improve it by any attempt at elaboration. In performance Cordelia is most effective when it is played directly, allowing the part to gain as much as it can by contrast with Goneril and Regan and the other villains of the play. This contrast is directly possible only in the first scene, but the dramatic effect of Cordelia's refusal to flatter her father is overwhelming, and a very few minutes suffice to establish her as courageous and affectionate beyond the common measure, in a world where those qualities are likely to prove dangerous. The character gains immeasurably by contrast with Lear's anger, and from his assertion that she was his favourite child [91], and although Cordelia disappears during the most violent part of the action it is by no means true that she

disappears from the minds of the audience, and it is
not the least tragic circumstance that when she appears
again it is too late to aid her father. The burden of
the acting in the infinitely pathetic scene in which Lear
dimly recognizes Cordelia is all upon the man, and
here, as in the Nunnery Scene in *Hamlet* and the
Murder Scene in *Othello*, the duty of the boy actor is to
subordinate himself to the more important player. In
the actor's expression he must 'support' him by
unobtrusively excellent acting which does not aspire
to shine on its own account. Nor is it wise to discount the effect of Cordelia's appearance after her
death, when Lear mourns for her so grievously; much
of Cordelia's character is established by what Lear says
of her, and by what the faithful Kent says in her
defence.

Goneril and Regan are two vigorously written and
active parts, requiring in performance a breadth of
style and a strength of personality which will enable
them to dominate the stage in some of their scenes, and
to make a strong showing in the scenes where they
engage in a clash of will with Lear, the part which
would naturally be played by the best actor in the
company. For this reason it seems probable that they
were played by boys or young men who had passed the
first boy actor stage and were sufficiently robust to
give the parts their proper strength. The difference
between a boy of fourteen and a young man of
twenty would be noticeable chiefly in an increased
emotional and physical resource, and this, combined
with a thorough training in women's parts, would

make Goneril and Regan suitable parts for the latter.

Goneril is remorseless and inhuman, and Regan is timid, but vindictive and petty. Both are seen first ministering to the inordinate vanity of their father, and, as soon as he has left the stage, they reveal their true depravity in a prose passage [92]. From this time onward they make no attempt to conceal their motives, but behave with consistent villainy. Goneril's behaviour toward Lear is cold and cruel, and Regan's small-souled and contemptuous, as is shown by her:

> Good sir, no more; these are unsightly tricks,   [93]

when he kneels to her. Both daughters are witnesses of Lear's violent outburst before he goes out into the storm [94], and together they seem to form an evil force which dominates the scene.

Another matter which is evidence that the roles of the sisters were played by young men is the part which Regan takes in the blinding of Gloucester, where, after the difficult moment in which she plucks his beard, which would require careful playing in order to keep it from being ludicrous, she snatches a sword and attacks the faithful servant, an act too vigorous for a young boy, as it would require great care not to turn the scene into mere blood-and-thunder melodrama. The dialogue, too, of the sisters' quarrel over Edmund [95] has a tone not common in boy-actor's roles, and this rises to a considerable dramatic height without any device being used to lessen the strain. The exchange between Goneril and Albany over the paper is

interesting because of her impudent and daring replies
and her despairing exit. The roles are of more than
common difficulty and they are written without any
of the usual devices to lighten the boy actor's task.

MACBETH

Lady Macbeth presents few difficulties in performance, and the writing of the part is designed to make it
as simple as is possible without forfeiting the dramatic
value of the character. It is unnecessary to suppose
that Lady Macbeth was played by a young man, for the
part is well within the scope of a boy actor of sixteen.
The character is presented in sections, each of which
reveal a new aspect of Lady Macbeth's consuming
ambition. She is first seen brooding over Macbeth's
news of the witches' prophecy [96], and here she has
the advantage of being alone on the stage, which
enables her to impress her character upon the spectators
without pause or hindrance, and is able to augment
her first effect by the second soliloquy. By the time
Macbeth arrives she has decided on her course of
action and her last line:

Leave all the rest to me,

clinches the impression she has created of overmaster-
ing ambition working in an unscrupulous nature. The
effect of her behaviour in the next scene is to add
treachery to her other qualities, for she greets the
unsuspecting Duncan with fair words. The actor is
not asked to reveal her duplicity by subtle means,

however, for the lines are written in perfectly straightforward fashion as those of a hostess welcoming a
royal guest. The impression of duplicity is given by
the memory of the preceding scene.

The scene which follows immediately upon Lady
Macbeth's welcome to Duncan shows her goading her
unhappy lord to the murder. Here the boy actor is in
the unusual position of being the active character in a
scene where the protagonist is passive. Macbeth,
however, is so much 'written down' in this scene that
Lady Macbeth has the advantage by sheer force of
words, as she spurs him on to crime. In the scene in
which the murder is actually committed she is not the
dominating character, although she continues in the
same hectoring tone; here Macbeth dominates the
scene and his terror is the most potent force in establishing its characteristic atmosphere, which culminates
in the knocking at the gate. Lady Macbeth is opposed
to him, rather as one theme is opposed to another in
counterpoint, and her boldness not only adds to her
own character but serves to set off the imaginary
terrors of her husband and to lend them a febrile
quality which they would lack otherwise.

When Macduff has proclaimed the news of Duncan's
murder, Lady Macbeth has a spectacular collapse [97],
meant to be prominently placed on the stage, as the
repeated adjuration, 'Look to the lady,' testifies. This
is an easy way in which to suggest overwrought nerves,
as it puts no very great strain upon the actor and causes
a considerable stir when it is effectively done.

The next scene, in which Lady Macbeth attempts to

K

quiet her husband's fears [98], is entirely dominated
by him, and it is possible that this is meant to illustrate
not only the falling-off of her influence, but also the
weakening of her resolve.   In the banquet-scene, however, she gives no sign of weakness, but rather assumes
again the ceremonious courtesy with which she greeted
Duncan, and her asides to her husband are in her first
domineering manner.   The exhaustion which attacks
Macbeth after the guests have gone is to some extent
reflected in her three brief lines, and, here again, the
boy actor is not meant to make himself unduly con-
spicuous while the chief actor is performing a difficult
feat.

The Sleep-Walking Scene, of which so much has
been written, presents no difficulties with which any
competent actor cannot deal successfully, and is so
skilfully written that no one to whom the part was
entrusted could possibly fail in it.   The Doctor and
the Gentlewoman make it plain to the audience that
Lady Macbeth is suffering under a mental strain which
drives her to walk in her sleep, and in their few
moments of brief expectant conversation they succeed
in establishing a strongly apprehensive atmosphere.
Before she speaks, Lady Macbeth has a short time in
which to suggest by dumb-show that she is in great
mental distress, and in this the comments of her
watchers assist her.   Mental illness always exerts a
strong fascination when it is shown on the stage, and
it is by no means difficult to simulate in its more
obvious forms.   The lines show clearly the direction
of Lady Macbeth's fears and anxieties, and the whole

scene can be played in a quiet key, with suitable
pantomime.   The scene is wonderfully effective in
performance, but the actress who says that it is extra-
ordinarily difficult must either be incompetent or
desirous of investing her part with a difficulty highly
flattering to herself.

It is interesting to observe that in most productions
of this play the actress who undertakes the part of Lady
Macbeth plays the Sleep-Walking Scene without any
regard whatever for the rhythm of her speeches, which,
although they are printed as prose, have a beat as com-   *
pulsive as any verse Shakespeare ever wrote.   Too
often these unobservant ladies strain and strive to
bring up tragic feeling from somewhere inside themselves, and completely neglect the strong hint which
the prose of the scene gives that it is to be played
andante con moto and without those pregnant pauses and
heavings of the bosom which would waken the most
determined somnambulist.   It is a theory of Mr Gordon
Craig's that all fine acting takes on the spirit of a dance,   *
and nowhere could this idea be better proven than in
the Sleep-Walking Scene.   Let the actress forget about
herself and her desire to do something new which
will win her the brief, gaping tribute of the uncritical,
and *dance* this scene, following the carefully planned
rhythms of the prose, and she will have a great success
with far less labour than if she tears herself to pieces
in the belief that she is giving richly of herself by so
doing.   It is always easier and more effective to act
with Shakespeare than to act against him.   A boy actor
who had been trained to follow the rhythm of Lady

Macbeth's lines could act rings around an actress who disregarded them in favour of an invention of her own. But the boy actors were musical and understood rhythm, and few actresses do, it appears.

ANTONY AND CLEOPATRA

In *Antony and Cleopatra* the parts of Iras and Charmian are of more interest than is usual in the subordinate women's roles in tragedy, and they are given an alteration or development of character, changing from the frivolous creatures of the early scenes to something like nobility when they choose to die.   Octavia is for many reasons an ungrateful role, for she is drawn to form a contrast to Cleopatra and so her nobility and dignity appear often as negative and uninspired.   In this play, where departure from the norm of virtue is exalted, Octavia and Octavius serve chiefly as contrasts to the passionate brilliance of the protagonists, and so they often seem dull and dreary, in their Roman integrity, compared with the libertines who are wrapped in a mantle of glory.

The role of Cleopatra is well within the technical and emotional scope of a boy actor of sixteen or seventeen years, but his approach to the part would be entirely the reverse of that commonly used by modern actresses. To an Elizabethan audience the circumstance of Cleopatra's royal station would be more significant than it is now, as the life of the nation was more intimately concerned with the patronage of nobility and royalty, and the warm glow of Tudor magnificence gave sovereignty a glory which it has never since recaptured. In presenting Cleopatra the boy actor would show her primarily as a queen, with a queen's dignity and poise, and his moments of levity and pettishness would be departures from this basic conception of the character.

The first entrance of the lovers, after the brief introductory speech of Philo, shows them in considerable state, and Cleopatra's dignity could be shown in action while her passion expressed itself in words, and in the second scene her rallying of Antony would gain greatly from her personal poise.

Perhaps the matter of Cleopatra's dignity needs further explanation. It is a comparatively modern idea that passionate love can only be represented successfully on the stage by undisguised voluptuous movement and action. Such methods are only fitting in plays written expressly for their exploitation, and are wholly unsuitable to poetic drama in which life is shown at one remove, and their application to it will have results which are either ineffective or nasty according to the resources of the actor. The union of dignity with beauty would give the actor of Cleopatra an enchantment far above mere sensual charm, and her passion would find its expression in her speeches. Dignity on the stage is the result of self-possession, and is a compelling and hypnotic quality, and is not to be confused with mere strutting prodigiousness.

Much of the love of Antony and Cleopatra is built up by inference and report. Cleopatra's lines describing past revelry with her lover are worth a whole scene of action, as when she cries:

That time? O times!
I laugh'd him out of patience, and that night
I laugh'd him into patience, and next morn,
Ere the ninth hour, I drunk him to his bed;
Then put my tires and mantles on him, whilst
I wore his sword Philippan,   [99]

and Enobarbus's description of the first meeting of the
lovers, coming early in the play [100], gives an impression of magnificent, overwhelming passion and of
superlative feminine magic which add immeasurably
to Cleopatra's character. It is true that the speech
would be mere anti-climax if the actor of Cleopatra had
not already made a deep impression on the audience,
and this again makes the approach by dignity and
suggestion a more effective one than that of volup-
tuousness and suggestiveness, as no ordinary mortal
could hope to fulfil objectively the woman of
Enobarbus's description.

The stressing of the royal side of Cleopatra's nature
would also make the scene of her attack upon the
Messenger [101] more credible than it would ordinarily
seem, for once he had made her royalty a strong factor
in the conception of Cleopatra's character held by the
audience, the boy actor could trade upon the prerogative of royalty to do strange and violent things. This
scene supplies one reason for assuming that Cleopatra
was played by a boy of sixteen or more, for a small boy
could not play it without seeming ridiculous, because
of the difference in height between himself and a man
of ordinary stature.

In the scene of Antony's death [102] the acting
burden is divided fairly equally between the two

protagonists, and there is no question of one being the
active and the other the passive party in it. After
Antony's death Cleopatra's grief is given expression in
two rhetorical passages [103] and also by the device of
a faint. The emotion contained in the speeches is of
the deepest and most exhausting kind, but the form in
which it is cast is of such singular beauty that the actor
need only give it appropriately beautiful utterance.
Interpretation in these speeches is better kept well in
control, and displays of personal feeling, as tears and
groanings, are more likely to harm the effect than to
help it. The beauty of the close of this scene lies in
the poetry, and it needs only to be spoken beautifully
and with simple sincerity.

In the last scene of the play an atmosphere of strong
tension is built up, and the whole burden of it falls on
Cleopatra, who is the active agent, confronted by a
number of opponents. The scene is a difficult one,
but the fact that her adversaries change is something of
an advantage, as it gives the actor of Cleopatra an
opportunity to build up a cumulative strength which
is allowed to no one else.

A passage in this scene which demands consideration
in this study is Cleopatra's bitter outburst:

> The quick comedians
> Extemporally will stage us, and present
> Our Alexandrian revels; Antony
> Shall be brought drunken forth, and I shall see
> Some squeaking Cleopatra boy my greatness
> I' the posture of a whore. [104]

One thing is perfectly certain; this speech is not intended to draw attention to any defect in the speaker,

for any such inopportunely ironic stroke would destroy the illusion of the play at the point where its maintenance was of the greatest importance. It is also possible to argue from the passage that the actor of Cleopatra had himself a low and beautiful voice. However, as the passage comes in the last Act of the play, when dramatic tension has reached a high point, it is unlikely that the audience would attach any significance to it other than that given by Cleopatra herself, one of revulsion and shame. In the excitement of the moment they would hardly connect the reference to the boy actor with the figure whom, for the previous four Acts, they had accepted as Cleopatra, nor, as the speech takes no more than fifteen seconds in delivery, would they have much opportunity to do so. It is far more probable that the excellence of the actor who played Cleopatra was such that this speech was introduced with the knowledge that, in the brief time the audience had to think about it, and in the exalted emotional context of the scene it would, in its audacity and irony, have a superbly dramatic effect.

It is not unlikely, also, that this speech may have had reference to a play on the Cleopatra theme in the repertoire of some rival company. This play could have been Samuel Daniel's *Cleopatra*, which first appeared in 1594 but was altered in 1607, and it is the opinion of Sir Edmund Chambers that these alterations were made with reference to Shakespeare's play. If this is so his irritation finds its vent in the bitter word 'extemporally' and in the taunt at the rival Cleopatra which is hurled from his stage. But only a good actor could speak these lines with impunity, and with the modern conception of Cleopatra the 'posture of a whore' is too often an unhappy reality which gives a new meaning to a passage which time has made unintelligible to a great part of any audience.

After this long and arduous beginning there are a few minutes of quiet relief in the passage with the Clown who brings the basket containing the asp, and then the scene rises to a sudden climax in the passage of Cleopatra's death. The concentrated passion of this scene makes heavy emotional demands upon the actor, but it is very brief, and here again speech must take precedence over any physical display in the representation of Cleopatra's mingled anguish and ecstasy at dying.

It cannot be said that in tragedy Shakespeare was ungenerous in the parts which he wrote for boy actors, for some of the tragic heroines are of first-rate importance, but it may justly be claimed that they are objective rather than subjective in their presentation. They are conceived and executed in simple terms and there is never the least doubt as to what they mean or what they are. They are never tortured by doubts either of themselves or of others, nor are they ever seen in a situation in which there is more than a nominal decision as to which course they shall take. Technical means, too, are used to simplify their task. The device of wearing boy's clothes is used to benefit Imogen as it was for the Julia of *Two Gentlemen of Verona*, to enable her to increase the pathos of her part

by using a boy's charm directly upon the audience,
rather than through the medium of a female impersonator's technique.   Juliet is supplied with several
long rhetorical speeches, some of them soliloquies, to
help her to establish a character by these comparatively
simple means.   The use of music gives a heightened
pathos to Ophelia and Desdemona.   But in no case
is a woman put in a position which requires not
merely simple emotion and an excellent technique but
subtle and subjective acting and the presentation of
a complex state of mind.

This point is best illustrated in the tragedies of
Hamlet and *Macbeth*.   The actor of Hamlet has a task
of remarkable complexity; he must show the nature
of a man who pretends to be mad, and yet is sane,
although he is labouring under a strain which at times
makes him hysterical and violent.   The struggle in his
soul is the matter of the play and his thoughts and
actions reveal a gradual and logical development in his
character.   Ophelia, on the contrary, is seen in static
emotional states; to begin with she is under no strain
and appears quite normal; she is later seen grief-
stricken because of her lover's ill-use of her; when last
she appears she is mad.   The changes are definite,
and the steps which lead from one to another are
omitted.

So it is in *Macbeth*.   The play shows in detail the
gradual deterioration of the hero's character and his
accompanying terrors and misgivings.   Lady Macbeth
is static; she appears first as a remorseless and ambitious
woman and of her decline nothing is shown until it is

an accomplished fact, and she is seen at last, haunted by the memory of a crime.

Shakespeare's tragic heroines are finely conceived and are executed with masterly technical skill, but the great moments of tragic passion and the speeches which go beyond the range of technique allied with good will are given to the heroes, for the actor of these would have the experience of life which brings ripeness and depth of emotion to the interpretive artist, enriches his imagination, and enables him to apprehend fully the work of the creator.

CHAPTER IV

The Old Women in Shakespeare's Plays and the Men who played them—The Children in Shakespeare—Unusual Roles written for Boy Actors.

THE number of boys who were permanently employed in an Elizabethan playhouse probably varied between three and five, and few plays demand more women than these could manage, if the minor parts were doubled. The two best boys would, of course, play the heroine and the second lady or confidante, and the others would make themselves useful in such parts as Mopsa and Dorcas in *The Winter's Tale* or Maria and Katharine in *Love's Labour's Lost*: sometimes they would have more important parts as heroines of sub-plots, such as Jessica or Anne Page. The parts of old women were played by men, who might double them with a male character, if the play permitted it.

The allotment of old women's parts to adult actors would be a satisfactory plan in a company where many of the players had been on the stage since childhood and had experience as boy actors behind them. Their performances were no doubt conventional, but that would not prevent them from being dramatically effective. Types of character seem to have been very arbitrarily differentiated on the Elizabethan stage, and it is noticeable that in Shakespeare's plays old age is frequently an attribute of a character whose children are still under twenty. Lady Capulet is old and so is

Polonius; the mother of Richard III is eighty although her son is a young man. There can be no doubt that these characters bore visible signs of age in performance, wore white hair, walked slowly and with a stoop, and probably caused their voices to tremble in their affecting speeches. These methods of representing age seem crude to-day, because they are generally employed and abused by bad actors, but they are perfectly adequate when skilfully used, and when the audience is prepared to accept them as symbols of age as a time of life rather than as a minute representation of the infirmities of any particular old person. The modern audience is keenly critical in matters of this sort, and perhaps rightly so; it is well to remember that the Elizabethan actor's idea of old age was no more ridiculous to his audience than the conventional clashing together of foils, which passes as a duel on our modern stage, would seem to Shakespeare's contemporaries.

The actors in children's companies had considerable experience in acting the parts of aged persons, and some of them were very clever in this sort of impersonation, as Jonson's *Epitaph* on the child actor Salathiel Pavy shows, but it is extremely doubtful if their performances would have carried conviction in an adult company, as their acting would be upon too small a scale. In Shakespeare's plays, also, he sometimes uses his old women characters to produce dramatic effects which are beyond the scope of the boy actor, and which lie in the province of the experienced adult. A child might, in a cast made up entirely

of children, give a satisfactory performance as Mother
Bombie in Lyly's comedy of that name, but Shakespeare's important old women are drawn on a different
scale, and an examination of them will show in what
direction they lie beyond the power of the boy
actors.

Such parts as the old gentlewoman, Alice, in
Henry V [1], and the old lady who attends Anne
Bullen [2], are probably introduced merely because
no boy was available to play them, though in both
cases the age of her companion would set off the charm
and beauty of the younger woman. The part of the
Duchess of Gloucester in *Richard II*, however, although
she appears in one scene only [3], has a place in the
scheme of the drama, and has some vigorous lines to
speak. The Duchess of York, in the same play, has
one scene in which she takes an active part in a passionate quarrel between York and Aumerle, and it is
noticeable that neither here nor in the subsequent
scene in which she pleads with Bolingbroke for her
son's pardon is the scene 'written down' for her
benefit. The part needs an actor who will seem
neither weak and ineffectual, nor too obviously acting
his hardest, but someone who can play as an equal
with York.

Similarly, in the second part of *Henry VI* the role of
Eleanor, Duchess of Gloucester, requires more robust
acting than a boy could give without too obviously
putting a heavy strain on his resources. The scene in
which she is struck by the Queen [4] needs a display of
violent temper imperfectly held in check, always a

difficult emotion to act without erring on either one side or the other, and the following scene in which she is apprehended while visiting the magician likewise requires a show of anger. The Duchess's career of misfortune continues with a trial [5] at which she is defiant, and then her public penance, after which she vanishes from the play. The part is carelessly written, and Eleanor's final repentant speeches are at variance with her unruly disposition as it has been shown earlier in the play. The small parts of the witch, Margaret Jourdain, and Simpcox's wife would also be played by men.

In *Richard III* the Duchess of York is eighty, and her chief purpose in the play is to join with Queen Elizabeth in her complaints against the cruelty of fate. Her great age, however, would gain sympathy for her from an audience in addition to what would naturally be felt for the mother of Richard. Her lines are somewhat formal, suiting the dignity of age, and fitting into the atmosphere of formally expressed grief in which the Queen moves. They speak with a regularity of rhythm and a passionless melancholy which gives their scenes a subdued tone, and in some places the pattern of speech gives the effect of a chorus [6]. The Duchess has a charming domestic scene [7] with her grandson, which soon changes to grief and provides her with an opportunity for a burst of strong emotion. At her next appearance she continues the strain of woe, and in her final speech:

Go thou to Richmond, and good fortune guide thee!
Go thou to Richard, and good angels guard thee!

Go thou to sanctuary, good thoughts possess thee!
I to my grave, where peace and rest lie with me! ..
Eighty odd years of sorrow have I seen,
And each hour's joy wrecked with a week of teen,

she has a mixture of adjuration to Dorset, Anne, and Elizabeth, and pathos evoked by her age and sorrow which combines to give her an exceedingly effective exit.

The part of Queen Margaret also was undoubtedly played by a man; the long speech of mockery in which she derides the unfortunate Elizabeth [8] is difficult to manage as it does not build up to any very remarkable climax, nor does it allow the actor to relax his effort at any time, proceeding very much on a level of sustained scorn. Both this part and that of the old Duchess are at once too difficult and too ungrateful to be given to boy actors.

Of the four female characters in *King John*, only Blanch of Spain would be played by a boy, and it is an insignificant decorative role. The part of Lady Faulconbridge is a small one, appearing only once [9] and having a few complaining speeches, similar in tone to those of the Duchess of Gloucester in *Richard II*. This is the sort of part which an actor of experience could combine with one or two other roles without the least inconvenience.

Queen Elinor is not a carefully drawn character and she vanishes from the action in the middle of the play. She is given several very definite and vigorous speeches, however, and indeed her part consists almost entirely of caustic interjections; her first speech is a testy

William Prynne, the Puritan; author of 'Histrio-mastix'

interruption of Chatillon and she continues in the same hectoring spirit until she dies and drops out of the action.

Constance is a more complete and living character than Elinor, although she too vanishes at the end of the third Act. Her grief, however, makes her an impressive and pathetic person, and the violence and bitterness of her complaint stamp her upon the minds of the audience so that she is remembered even when she is no longer seen, and contributes to the sum of John's evil-doing [10].

It is interesting to notice that Elinor and Constance, and, to a lesser extent, Lady Faulconbridge, are put in opposition to male characters who would be played by first-rate actors, and that in the conflict with these they take a very vigorous and active part. The conflict is between equal spirits, and in no case is the balance unfairly weighed against the male character. It is in this respect and also in the carelessness with which many of them are written, that Shakespeare's old women differ from his heroines and the parts written for boy actors.

In *Romeo and Juliet* Lady Montague is a shadowy character and was probably combined with one or two other roles by an actor who made himself generally useful. Lady Capulet has a part of minor importance, but she appears several times throughout the play, and her presence in the final scene is evidence that she was not doubled with another character, as Lady Montague is not at hand to 'balance' her, and she is not really necessary to the scene. She can hardly be said to

L

have any distinguishing characteristics at all, and is certainly not meant to be prominent in the play.

Dionyza, in *Pericles*, begins as a mere puppet, but later in the play she takes on a new importance and comes to life strikingly in the scene in which she tempts Leonine to murder Marina [11]; the prose in which she speaks has vigour, and when she speaks in verse to Marina there is individuality and strength to the lines. Similarly, in her dispute with Cleon she shows independence and a kind of robust lack of scruple which gives her considerable dramatic effectiveness.

Lychorida, the nurse, appears only in two scenes and a dumb-show, but the part demands a good actor, for the excitement of the storm-scene is great, and on the Elizabethan stage most of it would have to be suggested by the actors. Lychorida is an ungrateful and difficult part, demanding skilful and unobtrusive acting, and returning little applause.

The Queen in *Cymbeline* has some kinship with Dionyza. She is the stock character of the wicked stepmother, and in performance she requires a malignancy outside the usual scope of the boy actor. It is not the cold inhumanity of Goneril, but a meaner and more human quality of envy and hypocrisy which the Queen displays. There are lines given to the part which are so bad that it is obvious that no great subtlety was intended in the acting of it, as when she confides in the audience thus:

> Pisanio, thou that stand'st so for Posthumus!
> He hath a drug of mine; I pray his absence
> Proceed by swallowing that; for he believes

It is a thing most precious. But for her,
Where is she gone? Haply despair hath seiz'd her;
Or, wing'd with fervour of her love, she's flown
To her desir'd Posthumus: gone she is
To death, or to dishonour, and my end
Can make good use of either: she being down,
I have the placing of the British crown.

These may well have been among the thousand lines
which Jonson wished Shakespeare had blotted. The
Queen's long and statesmanlike reply to Lucius, the
Roman general [12], would require an authority in its
delivery unlike the quieter method of the boy actor.
The part was probably played by a man or a youth who
had passed his best days as a boy actor and was still
playing secondary women's parts from time to time.
The part of Hippolyta in *A Midsummer Night's Dream*
is another which would probably be assigned to an
actor of this class, as an Amazonian physique would
hardly be an attribute of a boy actor, and a mature man
would be too bulky and unattractive in the role.

In *The Winter's Tale* Paulina provides an important
and interesting part for the mature actor of female roles.
Paulina is carefully and vigorously drawn, and has the
sympathy of the audience from her first appearance.
She gets the better of Leontes in a very brisk quarrel [13]
and has a fine exit in the same scene. After the supposed death of Hermione it is she who brings Leontes
to his senses in a scene of remarkably eloquent verse
[14] and she appears again in the last Act to unite him
with his wronged queen. Paulina has remarkable
vitality and freshness, and has a part of first-rate
importance in the action of the play.

It is significant that in *Pandosto—The Triumph of Time*, by Robert Greene (1588), there is no prototype for Paulina, and the part may have been written for an actor who had unusual skill in parts of this kind.

The Countess of Rossillion, in *All's Well that Ends Well*, is a serious portrait of a dignified old noble-woman; in the play's source, which is Boccaccio's tale of *Giletta of Narbona* (*Decameron*, Nov. 9, giorn. iii), there is no original of this character and it is possible that this part also was written for some actor of particular skill. The part is by no means an easy one; no great variety of character is attempted, but the chief attributes of the Countess are the dignity and wisdom of old age. Her advice to her son [15] is reminiscent of that of Polonius, but is rather less disquisitional, and her conduct throughout the play is restrained and gentle. There is no opportunity for the actor to impress himself upon the minds of the audience save by skilful and sincere acting. Her first scene with the Clown [16] is charming, and the subsequent passage with Helena shows the kindliness of the old lady, but there is no chance for vigorous delivery or telling action, nor does any occur later in the play. The part, however, has a remarkable charm, and in the care of a good actor would make as deep an effect on the spectators as any in the play.

It is interesting to observe that the Countess opens the play. This difficult task is in no other case given to a female character by Shakespeare; they are rarely on the stage when the play opens, appearing only when the audience is quieted and in a receptive mood.

Another exacting role for the actor of old women's parts is that of Volumnia, the mother of Coriolanus. There is no other female role in the play which rivals it in importance; Virgilia is a lay-figure, a mere foil for Volumnia; she says little and weeps much. Valeria is in no way remarkable. Both the younger women are subordinated to Volumnia, a part second only to that of Coriolanus himself.

The actor who undertook Volumnia would in the first place have to assume the traditional dignity and nobility of the Roman matron. She is first seen in a simple domestic situation, sewing with her daughter-in-law, while Valeria gossips with them. Volumnia dominates the scene, which is no difficult task, as the two young women would probably be played by boy actors of no very great capacity. The scene in which Volumnia welcomes her victorious son is more taxing, for here the actor must show his joy and nobility with very little time in which to do it, and such a speech as:

> I know not where to turn: O welcome home:
> And welcome, general; and ye 're welcome all. [17]

requires a nice balance between the distracted rejoicing of a mother and the portentous dignity of a Roman matron which would be impossible for any one but a first-rate actor to hit. Her later reproaches to her son [18] must carry weight, and the actor must be of a quality to equal Coriolanus and Menenius. The final speech in which her pride rebels against that of her son is one of the most powerful climaxes in the play, and it demands an actor out of the common to lead up to it and to deliver it successfully. So, also, when Coriolanus is leaving Rome [19] in disgrace, Volumnia has to show heavy grief imperfectly controlled, which is made more difficult by her age; the tears of youth are comparatively easy to pump up on the stage, but the slower tears of old age are far harder to represent with any sort of artistic restraint.

Volumnia's last scene contains several technical difficulties. She has two unusually long speeches [20] which need deep sincerity in delivery; they cannot be declaimed with vigour, nor have they any beauties which allow of a poetic flight of elocution. The power required to give a blank verse speech of fifty lines without recourse to one or the other of these aids is not common, and would only be likely to be found in an actor of many remarkable gifts. The Folio stage-direction at the conclusion of the second of these speeches:

Holds her by the hand silent,

is significant testimony of the impression which the scene was intended to make, and also of a refinement of acting technique which critics who are loath to admit that what is old is sometimes good, attempt to deny to the Elizabethan stage.

Queen Katharine, in *Henry VIII*, first appears as a suitor to the King [21] on behalf of some of his subjects; as long as her petition is the chief interest of the scene she is the principal figure on the stage, and her direct attack on Wolsey must be made in such a way as to convey more of the antagonism between them than

appears in the words. Her later interjections on the
part of Buckingham also must be sufficiently pointed
to draw attention to Katharine's just and honourable
nature and its clash with the Cardinal's policy. These
incidents help to prepare for the scene of Katharine's
trial [22], in which, after a long and difficult speech in
her defence, she enters into a dispute with Wolsey and
administers at least one very sharp rebuke to him, for
when he urges her:

> Be patient yet,

she replies:

> I will, when you are humble, nay, before,
> Or God will punish me.

His reply to her is suave and reasonable, and her
rejoinder is strong and pointed; throughout the scene
Wolsey and Katharine are evenly matched, and there
is no attempt made to throw the woman's part into
prominence at the expense of the male character. The
same even division of acting opportunities exists in
Katharine's scene with Wolsey and Campeius [23],
neither of whom is 'written down,' although the scene
is as much between Katharine and the Cardinal as
though Campeius were not present. It is interesting
to notice that, although he is prominent in the dialogue of this scene, Campeius does not seem conscious
of the personal feeling between the Queen and his
companion.

The transition from the scene of Anne Bullen's
coronation procession to that of Katharine's death [24]
is strikingly dramatic. This is the only death-scene
given to a woman in any Shakespearian play, except

for those cases where women die by violence, where the technique is different. The pathos of the scene is remarkable, and Griffith's eulogy on Wolsey and Katharine's forgiveness of her enemy give a strong atmosphere of approaching death, when old enmities are forgotten. After the vision there is a technical difficulty in the Queen's rebuke to the impertinent messenger, which must be done with regal dignity but without forfeiting any of the sympathy of the audience. The scene is long enough for the actor to build up a powerful atmosphere, and he would need to take full advantage of it in the delivery of Katharine's last two speeches. The simplicity and pathos of these could only be successfully conveyed to his audience by an actor who could hold their undivided and sympathetic attention. The part of Katharine asks for an actor of first-rate technical and emotional power, not much below the performers of Wolsey and Henry in ability. The similarities in the demands made upon the actors of Katharine and Volumnia gives rise to some speculation as to whether the parts might not have been played by the same man.

It is easy to see in what respect such parts as the Countess of Rossillion, Volumnia, and Queen Katharine are unsuited to performance by boys, and what added opportunities were given the dramatist by the presence of experienced and adult actors of female roles. The parts which have already been discussed are of a serious and sometimes tragic nature, but Shakespeare further took advantage of this resource to introduce into several of his plays comic old

women's parts which add greatly to the variety of
their humour.

The comic old woman on the Elizabethan stage was
invariably a person in an inferior social position, or, in
the case of witches like Mother Sawyer, of no social
position at all.   Her humour was likely to be of a
broad and earthy nature, for the Mrs Mountstuart
Jenkinsons of Elizabethan life are never met with in
the drama, but it is none the worse for that, and has
endured in full colour when the witticisms of the
Princess of France have faded.   As parts to act they
are unsuitable for boys; there is a rich unction about
them only found in mature comedians.   A boy could
do wonders with the sharp wit of Beatrice or the warm,
sunny wit of Rosalind, but he would be inadequate for
the garrulities of Juliet's nurse.   There is a depth of
humour in Shakespeare's best comic old women which
must find a sympathetic response in the actor or he will
fail to do them justice, and this sympathy cannot be
expected in adolescents, who are usually more concerned with wit than humour.   It is unusual, also, for
actresses to play these parts satisfactorily, as they rarely
possess the necessary fund of jolly grossness and in
their struggle to achieve it they are sometimes vulgar
without being funny.   In this connection it may be
noted that when Jonson's *Bartholomew Fair* was revived
by the Phoenix Society in 1922 the part of Ursula the
Pig-woman, a part almost impossible to an actress, was
played with great success by Roy Byford, the celebrated
actor of Falstaff.

Certain actors no doubt specialized in parts of this

sort.   John Downes, in the *Roscius Anglicanus*, gives
the names of six actors who commonly acted women's
parts at the Cock-Pit in Drury Lane in 1659, and of two
of them he says:

> *Mosely* and *Floid* commonly acted the Part of a Bawd and
> a Whore.

Several old women's parts were also in the repertoire
of the celebrated comedian James Nokes, who in 1762
appeared as the Nurse in Nevil Payne's *The Fatal
Jealousie* and also as the Nurse in Otway's *Caius Marius*
in 1679, gaining for himself the nickname 'Nurse
Nokes.'   He also played Lady Beardly in D'Urfey's
The Virtuous Wife in 1679 and Megaera in the same
author's *The Banditti* in 1686.   Colley Cibber tells us of
Nokes:

> In some of his low characters, that became it, he had a
> shuffling shamble in his gait, with so contented an ignorance
> in his aspect, and an awkward absurdity in his gesture, that
> had you not known him, you could not believe that,
> naturally, he could have a grain of common sense.

Nokes was the last of the male actors of old women,
and the only one of whom any details are left us.

The part of the Hostess in the Induction to *The
Taming of the Shrew* is insignificant, but it would be
necessary for the actor to have an appropriate appearance for it.   The actor who played the Hostess would
doubtless play another part as well and a likely one for
him would be the Widow, which would leave him idle
during four Acts, when he might play Curtis or the
Haberdasher.

Mistress Overdone, in *Measure for Measure*, is not a

particularly funny character, but she helps to build up an atmosphere of evil by her matter-of-fact discussion with Pompey [25]. She and her companion, the Bawd in *Pericles*, would doubtless be remarkable for the grossness of their appearance and the harshness of their voices. As has already been said in the discussion of the play in Chapter III, the Bawd and her companions create a background of depravity against which Marina's purity shows as a striking contrast.

One of Shakespeare's best comic women is Mistress Quickly, who appears in three plays. In the two parts of *Henry IV* she is wonderfully alive and busy and has several fine opportunities for rich comic acting, as, for instance, in the scene where Falstaff impersonates the King [26] and his hostess is lost in mirth and admiration, breaking out with the memorable line:

O Jesu, he doth it as like one of these harlotry players as ever I see!

This is a sort of irony of which Shakespeare seems to have been very fond.

Mistress Quickly is one of Falstaff's best foils; his dispute with her over the shirts is one of his best scenes [27], and his forgiveness of her for wanting what is her own is one of his most magnificent impudences. Like all the other comic characters in the play, Quickly derives much from Falstaff, and feeds him with the stuff of which his greatness is made. Perhaps her best scene, however, is that in which she describes his death [28]. The role demands first-rate comedy acting in the two parts of *Henry IV*, but here

it needs treatment of a very different sort, for the
mingling of comedy and pathos, without overdoing
one or the other, is possible only to a first-rate actor.
It is in such lines as:

Nay sure, he 's not in hell: he 's in Arthur's bosom, if ever
man went to Arthur's bosom,

that the capabilities of the actor are severely tested, for
here he must be funny without exciting laughter, and
grief-stricken without casting too great a gloom over
the scene.

In *The Merry Wives of Windsor* Mistress Quickly, like
Falstaff, is considerably reduced, but her introduction
into this popular piece shows that she must have been
a popular character in the earlier play. Her most
striking transformation is in the final scene when she
appears disguised as, of all things, a fairy, and speaks
some uncharacteristic verse. Sir Hugh Evans is a
Welshman and Pistol loves any sort of pretence, so
that their flights of fancy are not surprising, but from
the unlettered and earthy Quickly such a passage as:

And *Honi soit qui mal y pense* write
In emerald tufts, flowers purple, blue, and white;
Like sapphire, pearl, and rich embroidery,
Buckled below fair knighthood's bending knee:
Fairies use flowers for their charactery,

is a decided surprise, and it is doubtful if any attempt
to speak it 'in character' would be at all successful.
It is unlikely, however, that the change would attract
much attention in the excitement of the action.

It is possible that the same man may have played the
part of Mistress Quickly in all the plays in which she

appears. In that case he must have been a valuable
and popular player, for the part needs skilled comic
treatment.

Doll Tearsheet is an interesting and mysterious
character, for while there is nothing to show that she
is not a young woman, the part requires a sort of acting
which would hardly be expected of a boy. It is
probable that she was played by a youth of perhaps
twenty years of age, who would have both the skill
in acting and the knowledge of a very sordid side of
life which are necessary to understand it. Doll's
important scene is that in the tavern at Eastcheap [29].
She appears drunk, and drunkenness is not an easy
condition to act unless the player is contented with
a mere crude staggering and rolling about. Such an
exhibition would be out of place in this scene, which is
carefully written and has a remarkably brilliant comic
atmosphere from beginning to end. The comedy,
however, is not of the obvious kind; if Falstaff, Dame
Quickly, Pistol, and Doll are presented merely as
agreeable funny people the true soul of the scene has
been missed. It is their roguery and disreputability
which mingle with their humour to give the scene its
pungent quality as does the decay in a ripe cheese.
Doll Tearsheet, if she is to take her proper place in the
plan of the scene, must be an out-and-out harlot,
drunken and surly, but big-hearted and still clinging
to some rags of gentility when she condemns Pistol
as 'the foul-mouthedst rogue in England,' only to
overwhelm him with lively abuse when he speaks to
her. Dorothy is beyond the understanding of a boy,

who would be likely to stress her external characteristics and miss entirely the side of her which prompts that:

I love thee better than I love e'er a saucy young boy of them all,

which, even if it may not be strictly true, is a generous statement and does credit to her heart.

Doll needs very skilful playing technically and a great deal of understanding of a kind which cannot be gained by mere persistent study of the lines. The actor who undertakes the part must be prepared to give a very complete picture of the woman in a comparatively short time, and to present Doll so that, when she is last seen in the hands of the beadles, she seems in her native element.

Juliet's Nurse is probably the most celebrated of Shakespeare's old women, and the part has remarkable variety and richness. At her very first appearance [30] she embarks on a stream of reminiscence concerning Juliet's childhood, her own dead child, and her late husband's much-cherished witticism. The character is taken directly from Broke's poem, in which she is even more long-winded, and Shakespeare, with a few magical touches, converts her maunderings into mellow humour. In one scene at least [31] the Nurse is an admirable foil to Juliet, for there can be no doubt that the constant change of tone on the part of the older actor gives remarkable intensity to the importunities of the younger one.

Perhaps the scene in which the character of the Nurse

is best revealed is that in which she urges Juliet to
marry Paris. Her worldly wisdom speaks thus:

> Faith, here it is,
> Romeo is banish'd, and all the world to nothing,
> That he dares ne'er come back to challenge you;
> Or, if he do, it needs must be by stealth.
> Then, since the case so stands as now it doth
> I think it best you married with the county.
> O, he's a lovely gentleman!
> Romeo's a dishclout to him: an eagle, madam,
> Hath not so green, so quick, so fair an eye
> As Paris hath. Beshrew my very heart,
> I think you are happy in this second match,
> For it excels your first: or if it did not,
> Your first is dead, or 'twere as good he were
> As living here and you no use of him.

This speech shows very clearly her lack of genuine
sympathy with her foster-child and the essential
shallowness and baseness of her own character,
although she is not an unkindly old woman. It is
this same shallowness which produces her burst of
foolish and noisy grief when Juliet seems dead. Both
these scenes are difficult, for the actor must be careful
not to alienate the audience too much in the first, nor
may he allow himself to be funny at the expense of
his fellow-actors in the second. It should be noted
also that in the first of these two scenes the Nurse's
baseness serves as an excellent foil to Juliet's fidelity,
and so is of great value to the younger player.

The Nurse is seen at her most amiable when she
carries Juliet's message to Romeo [32]. In this scene
her facetiousness and her garrulousness are amusing
without any unpleasant undercurrent, and she appears

simply as an amiable old go-between. The character
is comic all through the play but the Nurse's tarnished
worldly wisdom is not always acceptable, and the actor
must be careful to give this aspect of the character its
due without overstressing it. Perhaps the greatest
difficulty encountered by the actor of the Nurse is to
find the proper balance of his part with the others in
the play. Certainly it demands skilful playing, and
an actor of ripe humour and experience.

Having now exhausted the roles which Shakespeare
wrote for the mature actors of women's parts, some
attention must be given to those which he wrote for
beginners. In several of the plays there are parts for
children, and these would be played by the youngest
and smallest boys in the company. The children in
Shakespeare's plays are somewhat precocious, judged
by modern standards, but there is ample proof that in
the sixteenth and seventeenth centuries children were
expected to be acute and critical at a very early age.

The two children of Clarence are introduced into
Richard III [33], and produce an effect of pathos which
is valuable to the play. The daughter of Clarence is
the only little girl in Shakespeare's plays and her part
is an insignificant one. In the same play the fate of
the king's two sons is important in the action, and the
scene in which their uncle persuades them to go to
the Tower is one of the most moving in the play. The
mistrust which the young princes feel of their uncle,
and their inability to resist him, produce a profoundly
pathetic effect. The children's roles are not difficult,
however, and the sinister atmosphere is entirely the

work of Richard and his companions. The natural charm which most children possess on the stage would suffice to endear the Princes to the audience, and the acting of Richard would do the rest.

A child's part of a very different sort is that of William, Mistress Page's son, who appears in one scene only, to be questioned by his schoolmaster [34]. He is a laconic boy, and the scene was certainly not written for his benefit, as the chief humour of it lies in the misunderstandings of Mistress Quickly and the disgust of Sir Hugh. It is difficult to know why this scene is in the play at all, as it seems to have no purpose, and introduces a boy actor who does not otherwise appear.

One of the most delightful scenes in *The Winter's Tale* is that in which Mamillius begins his sad tale [35], which is never finished. The remarkable charm of this young prince has captured the affection of many writers on the play, and the well-known piece of imaginative criticism by Swinburne in *A Study of Shakespeare* (1880) contains many tender references to him. Perhaps the secret of Mamillius's enchantment is that he is very much a child. He does not make clever remarks, like Gloucester's young nephew of York, nor has he the contentious nature of Lady Macduff's son. His innocence is used with great skill to set off Leontes's rising anger [36], and the King's obvious love for his son gives depth to his own character and increases the pathos of his ready suspicion of Hermione.

The part asks very little in the way of acting. A child with a pleasing nature and the ability to speak

M

well would do it admirably, and would be certain to
take more than his share of the attention of the
audience.   The natural air of children on the stage is
always in striking contrast with the hard-won graces of
the adult actors, and the difference would be very great
on the Elizabethan stage.   There can be no doubt that
Mamillius appealed strongly to the audience and that
the pathos of his death added immeasurably to the
strange nostalgic charm of the play.

Falstaff's page, Robin, appears in three plays, and it
is probable that the part was played by the same boy
in each.   There can be no doubt that he was the
smallest boy in the company, in order to make a
contrast with his huge master.   He does not come on
the scene until the second part of *Henry IV*, when
Falstaff makes his diminutive size the subject of a string
of jokes, and thenceforth he is valiant in defence of his
master and incorrigible in his tormenting of Bardolph.

In *The Merry Wives of Windsor* Robin, like Falstaff
and all his dependants, suffers diminution, and serves
merely as a runner of errands, but in *Henry V* he comes
into his own and has a large and attractive part, for
a child.   He expresses no grief at his master's death
but goes off to the wars with Nym and Pistol and
his old enemy, Bardolph.   He has a remarkable soliloquy [37] in which he gives his opinion of his patrons;
it is not particularly involved or difficult but it is
interesting that a minor character, and a very young
actor, should be given so excellent an opportunity
to show his mettle.   He next appears as interpreter
between Pistol and a French prisoner [38], a part which

requires some ability to speak French, or else a sufficiently good ear to learn the words parrot-like; the latter suggestion is unlikely, however, as the office could easily have been given to another character. At the end of this scene he has another brief soliloquy and goes off to guard the luggage of the camp where, from Fluellen's report [39], he was killed. The part which began as a mere stage property to set off the size of Falstaff, achieves real significance in this last play.

Another page of some consequence is Moth, the attendant of Armado. He has more repartee than Robin, and is altogether a more important person in the play. The joke of his size is used for all it is worth ('Moth' and 'mote'), and particularly in the show of the Nine Worthies, where he presents Hercules. Moth has several excellent opportunities to distinguish himself, and the part requires a clever child, although it is well within the capacity of such a one. Children, if they can act at all, act superlatively well, often to the shame of their adult colleagues. In performances of *Love's Labour's Lost* Moth always stands out as one of its most interesting and amusing characters. The actor of Moth must be a singer as well, for he is Ver in the song which ends the play.

Undoubtedly the best child's part of all of Shakespeare is that of Arthur in *King John*. Queen Elinor is an old shrew, and Constance speaks little more than complaints until the audience is half inclined to say with Pandulph:

You are as fond of grief as of your child.
If the wicked king wronged her alone his villainy

would cause some natural disgust but nothing of the horror and pity which is aroused by the murder of her son.

The part is not a long one, but the value of a role on the stage cannot always be measured by the number of its lines, and whenever Arthur speaks he speaks to some purpose. The speech with which he greets Austria is [40] nobly direct, and at once enlists the sympathy of the audience; it is better that Arthur should say little during the rest of the scene, for a show of litigiousness on his part would lose much of the good will which his youthful appearance and his one good speech have gained. It is a curious fact that audiences prefer to see a child wronged rather than to have him argue his case like a reasonable human being.

Arthur's silence during the first three acts of the play gives added effect to his eloquence in the great scene in which he pleads with Hubert to spare his eyes [41]. There is in this scene, in a remarkable degree, the quality of intimacy; it is not tragic judged by strict standards, but it is wonderfully personal and in performance it is almost unendurably pathetic. It is also interesting technically, for here the child is the active party in the scene, and the man is passive. The situation, however, is so devised that there can be no fear of failure on the child's part; here gentleness is acting upon cruelty, and the gentleness of Arthur, with his:

When your head did but ache
I knit my handkercher about your brows
(The best I had, a princess wrought it me)
And I did never ask it you again. . . .

HISTRIO-MASTIX.

THE
PLAYERS SCOVRGE,
OR,
ACTORS TRAGÆDIE,

Divided into Two Parts.

Wherein it is largely evidenced, by divers *Arguments*, by the concurring Authorities and Resolutions of *sundry texts of Scripture*; of the *whole Primitive Church*, both under the *Law and Gospell*; of 55 Synodes and *Councels*; of 71 *Fathers and Christian Writers*, before the yeare of our Lord 1200; of above 150 *foraigne and domestique Protestant* and *Popish Authors*, since; of 40 *Heathen Philosophers, Historians, Poets*; of many Heathen, many *Christian Nations, Republiques, Emperors, Princes, Magistrates*; of sundry *Apostolicall, Canonicall, Imperiall Constitutions*; and of our owne *English Statutes, Magistrates, Vniversities, Writers, Preachers.*

That popular Stage-playes (the very Pompes of the Divell which we renounce in Baptisme, if we beleeve the Fathers) are sinfull, heathenish, lewde, ungodly Spectacles, and most pernicious Corruptions; condemned in all ages, as intolerable Mischiefes to Churches, to Republickes, to the manners, mindes, and soules of men. And that the Profession of Play-poets, of Stage-players; together with the penning, acting, and frequenting of Stage-playes, are unlawfull, infamous and misbeseeming Christians. All pretences to the contrary are here likewise fully answered; and the unlawfulnes of acting, of beholding Academicall Enterludes, briefly discussed; besides sundry other particulars concerning *Dancing, Dicing, Health-drinking, &c.* of which the *Table* will informe you.

By WILLIAM PRYNNE, *an Vtter-Barrester of Lincolnes Inne.*

Cyprian, De Spectaculis lib p. 244.
Fugienda sunt ista Christianis fidelibus, ut iam frequenter diximus, tam vana, tam perniciosa, tam sacrilega Spectacula: qua, etsi non haberent crimen, habent in se et maximam, et parum congruentem fidelibus vanitatē.

Lactantius de Verò Cultu cap. 20.
Vitanda ergo Spectacula omnia, non solam ne quid vitiorum pectoribus insidet, &c. sed ne cuius nos voluptatis consuetudo delineat, atque à Deo et à bonis operibus avertat.

Chrysost. Hom. 38. in Matth. Tom. 2. Col. 299. B. & Hom. 8. De Poenitentia, Tem. 5. Col. 750.
Immo verò, his Theatralibus ludis eversis, non leges, sed inquietatem evertetis, ac omnem civitatis pestem extinguetis. Etenim Theatrum, cum multa luxuriæ officina, publicum incontinentiæ gymnasium; cathedra pestilentiæ; pessimus locus; plus uniuersumque morborum plena Babylonica fornax, &c.

Augustinus De Civit. Dei, l. 4. c. 1.
Si tantummodo boni et boni Hi homines in civitate essent, nec in rebus humanis Ludi scenici esse debuissent.

LONDON,
Printed by *E. A.* and *W. I.* for *Michael Sparke*, and are to be sold at the B. e Bible, in Greene Arbour, in little Old Bayly. 1633.

The title-page of Prynne's great work. It contains one thousand-odd pages

is, dramatically, the stronger force of the two. The
boy actor here is under no necessity to keep up an
illusion of femininity; he can call upon all his stores of
emotion and use them directly upon the audience, and
if he plays with artistic discretion as well, the scene
cannot fail to be profoundly moving. The tenderness
which usually attaches to the female roles is here all
concentrated upon Arthur, and the pity which the
audience feels for his fate supplies an element in the
play which would otherwise be missing.

This detailed examination of the old women's parts
and the children's parts in Shakespeare's plays, repetitious and wearisome though it has been, is necessary
to a clear understanding of the function of the boy
actor in the Shakespearian company, representing two
extremes of his art. The beginner, if he were attached
to his master at an early age, say ten or eleven, would
no doubt make his first appearance as a page in the
train of some great nobleman, as a singer when a
chorus was wanted, or as one of the singing pages in
As You Like It, and as a fairy or any other small
creature that might be needed. Two boys are wanted
for the vision in *Cymbeline* and six for a vision in
Henry VIII, all expert dancers; the boys in *Cymbeline*
could not be very small, as they are meant to represent
warriors, but the dancers of Katharine's vision might
well be children.

Large numbers of children are needed in *A Midsummer Night's Dream* as fairies, and in *The Tempest* as
nymphs, dogs, and spirits. The circumstances under
which these plays were performed would ease the

strain on the resources of the company. If, as has
been suggested by Sir Edmund Chambers (*William
Shakespeare*, vol. i, p. 359), *A Midsummer Night's Dream*
was played at the wedding of Thomas Berkeley and
Elizabeth Carey at Blackfriars on 19th February 1594,
Sir George Carey's singing-boys would be available
to serve as fairies.   So also, if the presentation of *The
Tempest* was at the celebrations attending the betrothal
of Elizabeth of Bohemia (1613), there would be no
difficulty in securing the services of royal choir-boys
for the masque.   It is possible also that one or two
boys from the company were placed among the pressed
men in order to give them cues for movement and
song, just as one or two experienced actors are placed
in a crowd of supernumeraries to lead them in their
part of the play.

The boy who was a satisfactory 'extra' would soon
be given small parts to play, perhaps those of children,
or Moth, Robin, or Fleance.   It is unlikely that there
would be more than two boys in this beginner stage at
one time, as the company would not want to pay out
money for a boy who was of very little use.   For this
reason too his progress would be rapid, and if he
showed himself talented he might have small female
roles allotted to him when he was twelve.   From this
time his advancement would depend upon his talents,
and would last as long as he was able to play women's
parts.   But when he was an adult actor regularly
playing roles requiring skill and responsibility, his
experience as a boy would make it possible for him
to give very convincing representations of old women,

and such roles as Volumnia and Queen Katharine would naturally come his way, nor are they parts which an actor would despise.

Perhaps the most difficult stage in the actor's life would be that during which he was neither boy nor man, but his training would dispose of the awkwardness which usually accompanies adolescence, and he would be able to play such parts as Mistress Ford and Mistress Page, or of Guiderius or Arviragus in *Cymbeline*, who are unable to sing. Guiderius is the elder of the two, and Arviragus is sixteen, and probably would be played by a boy a year or so older. Half-grown boys would likewise serve as the Reapers and perhaps as the Nymphs also in *The Tempest*, and as the Fiends who visit Joan la Pucelle and refuse to accept her soul.

It would be interesting to know precisely how the groups of extra players necessary for such spectacles as the ball-scenes in *Romeo and Juliet* and *Much Ado About Nothing*, the country dance in *The Winter's Tale*, and the coronation procession and the scene of Princess Elizabeth's christening in *Henry VIII* were hired, but there is little definite information on the subject. Doubtless there were plenty of unemployed actors who were glad to serve in these capacities, and these might have boys under their authority who would serve as partners in the dances. It is extremely unlikely that any great number of boys was kept on the payroll of the company merely to serve as supernumeraries.

Special talent would be required in a boy who was

chosen to play such a part as Titania; not only would
he have to be small and graceful but he would need
a particularly distinguished elocution to carry him
through a long and involved speech such as her
reproach to Oberon at their first meeting [42]. It is
probable that a very grand manner of acting was
assumed by Titania and Oberon, much resembling
modern ballet, and drawing heavily upon their own
skill as dancers. Such a formalization would serve to
distinguish their scenes from the romantically acted
passages between the lovers, and the comic acting of
the clowns. The part of Oberon would be thoroughly
suitable for a boy actor who had passed his best days as
a female impersonator but who had added experience
to his former grace and address. The tasteless custom
of casting a woman for this part is ridiculous and
destructive to the fabric of the play.

It is undoubtedly a fact that the fairies and super-
normal beings who appear in modern productions of
his plays are very different from the ones conceived by
Shakespeare. His fairies have more than a touch of
malice in them, and a profound determination to have
things their own way. Boys would play such parts
with gusto, and would give an impression worlds
away from the modern 'fairy ballet' in *A Midsummer
Night's Dream*. The Witches in *Macbeth* would appear
on the Elizabethan stage as realistic old crones, and
three good actors would use all their skill to give them
a lifelike presentation. It needs imagination to play
a fairy or a witch in broad daylight, and the Elizabethan
theatre must have been a great breeder of imagination,

for nothing daunted it, and not merely Oberon and Titania, but Caliban, Puck, and Ariel walked its enchanted stage.

The skill of the boy actor as a dancer and gymnast would be put to a severe test in the roles of Puck and Ariel. The modern custom of having these parts played by a girl is a detestable one, sentimentalizing and vulgarizing two of Shakespeare's most remarkable creations. Puck is a spirit of mischief, not absolutely dissociated from malice, of remarkable wisdom and curiously primitive and godlike in his understanding of, and lack of sympathy with, human frailty. Puck is the link which joins all the unrelated elements of the play together; although he stands outside and above it, he is the spirit of the fantasy, and the full flavour of the play is lost unless he is played by an actor who knows what Puck is, and has the technical skill to embody his knowledge in his performance.

So also it is with Ariel, for here the actor must represent an idea, or a group of ideas, which he can only do if he has the physical grace to give the part complete ease and impersonality. Ariel is 'an airy spirit' and the part must be played with aloofness if it is to take its proper place outside and above the rest of the cast. It is in these two unusual conceptions that Shakespeare puts the heaviest demands upon his boy actors, and that such parts should have been written for them is a remarkable testimony to the excellence of their art.

CHAPTER V

Indecency of Speech among Shakespeare's Women and its Effect on Audiences subsequent to the Restoration—Physical Love-making on the Elizabethan Stage with reference to the Boy Actor—The Technique of the Boy Actor as it affects the modern Actress in Shakespeare

AN attempt to estimate the extent to which Shakespeare's dramatic technique was influenced by the convention of the boy actor would be incomplete without some consideration of the indecency of speech which characterizes and, for some critics, mars many of his female characters. It has been suggested that this may be attributed to the coarseness of speech which was common in his age, but this is only a partially satisfying explanation, for Shakespeare's plays do not purport to be reflections of his time as do those of the satirist Jonson, and such topical references as occur in them are incidental to the plot, and not the chief matter of it.

There is a good deal of indecent speech in most ages, and whether it finds itself a place in the drama, and the extent to which it does so, depends not upon the wishes of dramatic authors but upon public taste. The chief difference between the indecency of the Elizabethan drama and that of the Restoration is that the former is frank and inclusive, and is not the attribute of any single class of characters, while the latter is confined almost entirely to sexual references,

is thinly veiled with modesty, and is the preserve of
the fashionable world.   Indecencies of speech occur
very rarely in Restoration tragedy: Cleopatra's banter
with the eunuch Mardian has no counterpart in
Dryden's play on the same theme; in Shakespeare's
tragedies and comedies alike he is apt to insert a coarse
line or two.   They are quickly gone, however, in most
cases, and herein his work differs from that of the
Restoration writers of comedy, whose chief plot and
source of wit was sexual irregularity.   The Shakespearian attitude toward indecency is one of frank
enjoyment, whereas that of Restoration comedy is
always one of tasting forbidden fruit, and it is significant that while Rosalind and Portia are not above
a broad joke, and seem none the less virtuous for it,
the heroines of the Restoration are too pure for any
such indulgence, which is left to the married women
of the plays.   There can be no doubt that Shakespeare
thoroughly enjoyed a dirty joke, but it was not the
only kind of joke he enjoyed; Restoration comedy
has one favourite joke, and it is harped on at the
expense of other sorts of humour.

Shakespeare's indecencies are not exclusively concerned with sex.   His strong-stomached audiences had
a childish relish for coprology, and Falstaff's inquiries
about his water in the second part of *Henry IV*, and his
command to the tapster to 'empty the jordan' would
give them a pleasure which a modern audience might
feel, but would be unwilling to express.   Sometimes
he is guilty of obscenity for its own sake, as in the
scene in *Henry V* in which the Princess Katharine is

given a lesson in English; this is no more than a smutty story, elaborated and drawn out until it reaches a climax which must seem a poor one to any audience which is not convinced that the mispronunciations of foreigners are very funny. Nowadays this scene is often played 'straight,' whether from excess of modesty or mere lack of comprehension on the part of the actors it is impossible to say; treated thus it falls flat. Sometimes it is played with the obscenities carefully pointed; this also falls flat as a usual thing. The scene would prove popular in Elizabethan England because jokes against the French were always welcome and because audiences of that day were doubtless more appreciative of that simple form of wit in which an innocent person is inadvertently the author of an obscenity.

There can be no doubt that the convention of the boy actors allowed Elizabethan dramatists a greater freedom to introduce passages of indelicate speech into their plays than that which has been permitted subsequently. Making full allowance for the manners of the time, it is unlikely that a gentleman in Elizabethan society would make such a reply to a lady as Petruchio does on one occasion.

Pet. Who knows not where a wasp doth wear his sting?
  In his tail.
Kat.   In his tongue.
Pet.   Whose tongue?
Kat. Yours, if you talk of tales: and so farewell.
Pet. What, with my tongue in your tail? Nay, come again,
  Good Kate, I am a gentleman.

This remark would pass as mere witty repartee, by

virtue of the patent artificiality of the situation.   An
attempt has been made in Chapter I to decide what sort
of illusion prevailed in the Elizabethan theatre, and if
the conclusions there are valid it follows that such a
repartee as the one referred to above would be unlikely to be regarded as more than a good joke.   It was
the greater objectivity of the Elizabethan stage illusion
which made possible such scenes as that in *All's Well
that Ends Well*, where Helena, immediately after a
soliloquy in which she confesses her love for Bertram,
is used merely as a foil for Parolles, feeding him with
questions as he gives a harangue about virginity.   No
subsequent dramatist could dare to use his leading
actress as a foil to the comedian, nor would he follow
her confession of love with a scene in which she takes
part in a rather questionable colloquy.

Although they may offend modern taste the fact that
Shakespeare gives indecent speeches to his heroines is
conclusive proof that he had no doubt of their suit-
ability and dramatic effect, and those who attempt to
give a subtle reason for their presence attach more
importance to them than their author did.   Mr Harley
Granville-Barker, in his discussion of the character of
Portia in the second series of his *Prefaces to Shakespeare*,
has a parenthetical passage, as follows:

(she jokes without embarrassment about taking the mythical
Balthasar to her bed, but she snubs Gratiano the next
minute for talking of cuckoldry, even as she snubbed
Nerissa for a very mild indelicacy—she is fond of Nerissa,
but no forward waiting-woman for her!)

Anything   that   Mr   Granville - Barker   says   about

Shakespeare in the theatre is likely to be of the very first importance, but in this, surely, he is mistaken. Her snub to Gratiano consists only of:

> Speak not so grossly,

which need not be interpreted as a reproach, and indeed in the context it seems far more likely to be a continuation of the joke. The snub to Nerissa, who has asked:

> Why, shall we turn to men?

is:

> Fie, what a question's that
> If thou wert near a lewd interpreter!

which is hardly a snub at all, for any indelicacy in Nerissa's speech is underlined by Portia's reply, which is surely meant to be humorous. Portia's part in the last scene of the play makes it perfectly clear that she has no objection to broad humour, and indeed relishes it; she would present a very unsympathetic picture on the stage if she were played as a woman who forbade licence of speech in others, while using it herself. It is unnecessary to whitewash Portia, for her real purity is so apparent that her occasional indelicacies seem only the natural result of a brilliant and inclusive wit.

Similarly, it is wasted effort to seek far-fetched explanations of the occasional indelicacy of Rosalind and Celia or to overburden with excuses Lucetta's joke about the codpiece, which in performance takes less than ten seconds, and is worth no longer consideration. The simplest and probably the truest way of accounting for the presence of these passages which are not to the modern taste, is to say that Shakespeare's audiences enjoyed indecent humour and that he, being no Puritan, indulged them from time to time; this still leaves the disparity between Shakespeare's indecent passages and those in modern drama unaccounted for, and the convention of the boy actor may be regarded as directly responsible for it.

The indecency of the drama since the appearance of women on the stage has been almost exclusively concerned with sex, and although the frankness of the Elizabethans may be uncongenial to some, it will scarcely be argued that the innuendoes and ambiguities of Restoration and much subsequent drama are less likely to corrupt those spectators who are so weak as to attach importance to them, or are more calculated to increase the self-esteem of the players who speak them. The sexual references and obscenities in Shakespeare are entirely frank and, even when disguised as word-plays, their purpose is never in doubt; in later drama this is not the case, and half the pleasure of the spectators at a modern farce lies in the apprehension of indecency, sometimes where none exists. The Shakespearian heroines make remarks which would certainly not be acceptable in any modern play, and yet they continue to give an impression of modesty and chastity, whereas a comparatively mild joke from the heroine of a modern comedy causes a disproportionate response from the audience, the members of which hasten either to be affronted or extravagantly amused. The reason for this is obvious to any one who has had any practical connection with the theatre,

N

or has been forced to calculate the response of an audience at any sort of entertainment in which men and women are equally concerned. The personality and beauty of a leading actress are certain to beget in the male half of the audience a concern for her which is partially directed at the character whom she represents and partially at her as a popular favourite. This duality of personality is shown with admirable clarity by the more unsophisticated members of a cinema audience who, when describing the plot of a film, very frequently speak of the heroine by her own name rather than that of the character whom she represented. This personal interest is almost equally strong, although less readily confessed, among the members of the audience at a play. From the time of Pepys the personal attractions of an actress have always rivalled those of the character she played, often with disastrous results to the latter.

This tendency on the part of modern audiences to concern themselves with actresses as people as well as characters in a play accounts to a very large extent for the changed attitude toward obscenity on the stage, and another important factor in the matter is the change in the social and moral outlook of the audience itself. Before the Restoration the audience at the playhouse consisted chiefly of two elements: the first of these was the groundlings who were pleased accordingly as the play gratified their simple desire for violent action, broad comedy, flaming words, or patriotic drum-beating; the second was the gentlefolk who judged the play by classical standards if they were scholars, or by

Parker.

fashionable standards if they were wits. Neither of
these elements was concerned about morals: the first
wanted excitement, and the second a more refined
aesthetic gratification; the first, despite the Reforma-
tion, was Catholic in its attitude toward right and
wrong; the second, with its Renaissance ideal of the
free individual, strove to recognize no barrier between
right and wrong. Together they did not form an ideal
audience for a poet, but they were infinitely preferable
to that which was to be his lot when the Puritans began
to be theatre-goers.

The Puritan influence on the theatre began as soon
as plays were revived in 1661. Although it is common
to think of the Restoration as a period of licence it was
so largely as a revolt against Puritanism, and the latter
force won the day. When the first bitterness had
passed away, and society had shaken down peacefully,
the influence which the shopkeeping and merchant
class had gained under the Commonwealth was clearly
evident, and in the theatre no less than in the world of
business. The Puritanism which rebuked the excesses
of the Restoration Court was the Puritanism of a large
and well-established middle class rather than that of a
comparatively small band of fanatics, as had been the
case in Shakespeare's day. This new theatre-going
class was distinctively Protestant, with all the Protestant concern for the moral responsibility of the
individual and the Protestant brand of introspection,
and the Protestant, as opposed to the Catholic, hypocrisy. It was a class ignorant of aesthetics and
suspicious of passion, and as its power grew it evolved

its own aesthetic standards and its own notion of the permissible aspects of passion and imposed these upon the theatre.

To such an element in the audience, the obscenity of Shakespeare's women would be unbearable. As the playgoers would not wish to hear their wives or daughters making directly indecent jokes, so also they deplored it in stage heroines; as they could not believe in the chastity of a woman who was given to occasional lewd speech in real life, so they applied this criterion to the women of the stage. Indeed it may be said that they still do so, for a large part of almost any audience in England or America to-day has a Protestant Puritan background, however much it may be grimed over, and the League of Decency organized by the Roman Church is in many of its aspects borrowed from Protestantism.

These two elements, the identification of the actress with some loved object, whether real or ideal, and the Hebraic rather than the Hellenic attitude toward works of art, have combined to cloud the general conception of Shakespeare's women and to make their looseness of speech a blot upon their character rather than an integral part of it. Of the first of these elements the Puritans were warned by Prynne as early as 1632:

> With what eyes then canst thou now behold thy wife, which thou hast there seene prostrated to so great an iniury in the person of another? How canst thou refraine from blushing, as oft as thou remembrest thy wife, when thou shalt there see the same sex so filthily made common?
>
> (p. 405.)

The second of these elements has resulted not only in
hundreds of tendentious plays and dramatized sermons
but has also attracted unnecessary attention to the
private lives of actresses. It is a Protestant Puritan
notion that the good artist must also be a good man.
They demand therefore that actresses in Shakespeare
must be good women because they perform in great
plays, though the universal attraction of wickedness
makes scandal about an actress a tasty morsel even to
the Puritan, and actresses of no great talent from Nell
Gwyn to Ada Isaacs Mencken (to come no nearer
our own day) have thriven by their evil reputations.
On the whole, however, the public likes to make
goddesses of its actresses and to see in these all the
beauty and romance which life does not give the
average theatre-goer, and to the Puritan playgoer who
makes a goddess of an actress it is unendurable that
Shakespeare should make her talk bawdry, for this
either disgusts him or awakes in him feelings which
perhaps he dare not acknowledge even to himself.
For these reasons, also, he cannot watch those scenes
in *Titus Andronicus* in which Lavinia appears mutilated,
or those in *Pericles* where Marina is kept and tormented
in the bawdy-house at Mytilene.

This tangled psychological jungle did not threaten
Shakespeare's freedom when he wrote parts for his
boy actors. The chief interest of the audience centred
upon the character the boy played, rather than upon
himself, and such personal interest as they took in him
was usually concerned with his skill as a female
impersonator, for the boys cannot always have stood

in such moral jeopardy as the Puritans imagined. There can be little comparison for the average spectator between the direct charm of an actress and the purely professional graces of a boy actor; in the former her direct sexual attraction gives a peculiar enchantment to the woman's performance, and in the latter this important element is lacking, and as sex is a quality common to all men and a nice aesthetic discrimination is the attribute of the few, the actress must always win the day, and the philosophers of art such as Goethe and Mr Gordon Craig must always lose it.

It is an attribute of genius that it takes full advantage of circumstances and Shakespeare uses the impersonal quality in the boy actor's art to achieve effects which are not duplicated in any drama written since women appeared on the stage. Reference has already been made to the curious effect achieved in the brief passage in *Hamlet*, where Ophelia is insulted in public by her lover. In these lines, which are usually cut in modern productions, Shakespeare uses indecent speech to produce a tragic, or at least pathetic effect; Hamlet, for his own reasons, chooses to perplex and mock at the lady who loves him. These lines, if they were not cut or hurried over, would prove almost unbearable on the modern stage, where Ophelia's pain would be felt too keenly. On the Elizabethan stage the effect of this passage would be realized fully, without a disturbing sense of being personally implicated.

Similarly, the scene in *Henry IV* in which Doll Tearsheet makes her first appearance cannot be given its full value in modern productions, for Doll is a harlot

A contemporary wood-cut of a scene from Kyd's 'Spanish Tragedy,' showing a boy actor as Bel-Imperia. He is believed to be the celebrated Nathaniel Field

of no very refined type, and there is a bitterness
beneath the humour of the scene which is much like
that which prompted the famous Sonnet cxxix. A
woman cannot usually act Doll, for she will either try
to stress the good points of the character unduly or will
give the woman's depravity a personal colour which
robs the scene of its humour. A boy could act Doll
admirably, for he could be perfectly abandoned and yet
remain sufficiently aloof to rob the portrait of its
particularity. It is necessary only to present an
audience with the outward form of a character like
Doll, and if this is done completely and successfully,
the audience will supply the rest of it, each from his
own imagination, and as his imagination or experience
is rich or poor, so will be his understanding and
appreciation of her nature.

If Shakespeare's stage had not been occupied by men
alone it is doubtful if he would have made Lear say:

Behold yon simpering dame,
Whose face between her forks presageth snow,
That minces virtue, and does shake the head
To hear of pleasure's name;
The fitchew nor the soiled horse goes to 't
With a more riotous appetite.
Down from the waist they 're Centaurs
Though women all above:
But to the girdle do the gods inherit,
Beneath is all the fiends';
There 's hell, there 's darkness, there 's the sulphury pit,
Burning, scalding, stench, consumption, fie, fie, fie! pah,
   pah! Give me an ounce of civet, good apothecary, to
   sweeten my imagination: there 's money for thee.

In a theatre where men and women mix on equal

terms certain courtesies must be observed, and where
courtesy reigns unpalatable truths may not be spoken.
The introduction of actresses upon the stage enriched
the drama in some respects, but in others reduced it to
beggary, for aspects of human nature which are not
congenial to women or which reflect too grossly upon
them have no longer a place in popular drama.

Another aspect of the art of the boy actor which must
be considered here is that dealing with physical love-
making on the stage, and the extent to which the
convention controlled it. Mr Harley Granville-Barker
is convinced that it was reduced to a bare minimum,
and in an essay on *Shakespeare's 'Dramatic Art'* (in
A Companion to Shakespeare Studies, 1934) he says that
the dramatist 'never set the boy to do anything
ridiculous or embarrassing.' A judgment such as this,
coming from a critic who is also a distinguished man
of the theatre, seems puzzling, for Mr Granville-
Barker is well aware that the first duty of an actor is
to overcome his self-consciousness and to do anything
that is demanded of him without embarrassment, an
emotion which rapidly spreads to the audience and
ruins dramatic illusion. Embarrassment would be
natural in an untrained boy, and his response would
probably be ridiculous, but the rigorous training which
has been described in Chapter I would soon fit the boy
actor for this part of his task, as well as for many others.
If a boy found his work embarrassing it is unlikely
that he would make very much progress on the
stage.

Mr Granville-Barker in his discussion refers chiefly

to *Romeo and Juliet* and to *Antony and Cleopatra*: he concludes his treatment of 'The Boy as Woman' thus:

> Cruder phases of the emotional traffic between male and female his audience must take for granted; he can make no effective play with them. But what of true tragedy, or comedy, or even of the finer savour of romance, rests in these? Very little; and in that little still less variety. Shakespeare goes clean to the heart of romance. From a canoodling Romeo and Juliet, from the calf-love for Rosaline on exhibition, God preserve us!—do we not so exclaim if we imagine the sort of thing and compare what we have in its place?

It is undoubtedly true that in many productions of *Romeo and Juliet* and of *Antony and Cleopatra* the plays are vulgarized and debased by the crass conceptions of producers and actors who are lacking in taste; they overload the love-scenes with action and destroy the balance of the plays. It is simply not true, however, that Shakespeare's plays, as performed in his day, were scamped as regards the presentation of physical love-making. Audiences have always, and quite rightly and understandably, been interested in love-scenes, and will not continually be fobbed off with poetry, however great it is. Audiences will accept a great deal of shadow but they demand a little substance as well, and Elizabethan drama has plenty of scenes in which a certain amount of physical love-making must be introduced to give life to the verse. In the popular *Spanish Tragedy* this scene occurs between Horatio and Belimperia:

Bel. If I be Venus, thou must needs be Mars;
And where Mars reigneth, there must needs be wars.

Hor. Then thus begin our wars: put forth thy hand,
That it may combat with my ruder hand.
Bel. Set forth thy foot to try the push of mine.
Hor. But first my looks shall combat against thine.
Bel. Then ward thyself: I dart this kiss at thee.
Hor. Thus I retort the dart thou threw'st at me.
Bel. Nay, then to gain the glory of the field,
My twining arms shall yoke and make thee yield.
Hor. Nay, then my arms are large and strong withal:
Thus elms by vines are compass'd, till they fall.
Bel. O, let me go, for in my troubled eyes
Now may'st thou read that life in passion dies.
Hor. O, stay a while, and I will die with thee;
So shalt thou yield, and yet have conquer'd me.

Surely this scene might justly be described as 'canoodling'?

There is plenty of evidence that such scenes as this one were presented with realistic action. The Puritans feared its influence on the spectators, and as usual the invaluable Prynne has his say:

Hee who shall but seriously consider those amorous smiles, and wanton gestures; those lascivious complements, those lewde adulterous kisses and embracements; those lustfull dalliances; those impudent, immodest, panderly passages; those effeminate, whorish, lust inflaming sollicitations, those several concurrences, combinations, conspirations, of artificiall, studied and more then Brothel-house obscenities: *those reall lively representations of the acts of venery*, which attend and set out stage-playes; must needs acknowledge that they are the very *Schooles of baudery; the Tutors, the occasions of reall* whoredomes, incests, adulteries, &c.

The kisses in Shakespeare's plays range from the commonest courtesies, such as Falstaff's greeting-kiss to Mistress Ford, whom he scarcely knows, and Lord Sands's kiss given to Anne Bullen at Wolsey's banquet,

to the passionate embraces of Antony and Cleopatra.
Of these latter the first has been a matter of dispute
among critics, as the stage direction for it does not
appear in the earliest texts of the play (Pope was
the first editor to introduce the stage direction
'embracing'), but it has some justification on the
stage, for it endorses the account of Antony's infatuation with which Philo opens the play and gives the
audience a physical demonstration of it which they
expect and without which the passion of the lovers will
seem less real to them. The second is the 'soldier's
kiss' before battle, and the last the one or many kisses
which Cleopatra gives when Antony is dying. It is
probable that on the Elizabethan stage such embraces
as the first two of these would be performed with
formal grandiosity, to be in accordance with the
Renaissance idea of heroic greatness, but the fact
remains that the kisses are necessary to the action and
cannot be avoided.

By no means all the kisses of Shakespeare's lovers
are on so grand a scale as these, however. Proteus and
Julia are not heroic figures, and in the scene in which
she gives him a ring as a keepsake they kiss, and
because of the nature of the scene, which is intimate
and tender, the acting and the embrace would doubtless be naturalistic in technique. So also would that
with which Bassanio claims Portia as his betrothed
wife. The romantic plays of Shakespeare do not
demand the same sort of magnificent acting as the
tragedies and the passion of the lovers in the romances
and the comedies can hardly have been presented in

so exalted a manner. Even the witty Beatrice and Benedick have a kiss in the last scene of *Much Ado About Nothing*, and a kiss, moreover, which is given special importance by a technical device. In a previous love-scene Beatrice has refused to kiss Benedick, and if she did not do so before the play was ended it is extremely likely that the audience would feel a dissatisfaction which, although they might not realize it fully, was caused by this omission. The kiss which unites them at the end of the play, however, gains strength and significance from the previous disappointment, and gives great dramatic value to the final capitulation of Beatrice. The method by which Shakespeare achieves this effect is analogous to the musical device called a 'disappointed climax' whereby the composer gives added value to a resolution or modulation by approaching it once without completing it, only to return later to achieve a satisfactory conclusion.

It may seem that this discussion attaches too much importance to kisses in Shakespearian drama, but on the stage a kiss has a value as a sign of love which must not be underestimated. The makers of films, who so frequently end their entertainment with a picture of hero and heroine in a prolonged embrace, understand very well the significance which it conveys to the audience. A kiss, in Shakespearian drama, is likely to represent a love-vow which must not be broken, if it is not clear from the context that it is merely a courtesy. It is the frequent kisses of Troilus and Cressida which gives their love intensity and which makes her final apostasy so shocking. Even in poetic drama actions speak louder than words, and when Cressida bestows on the Grecian generals the favours which Troilus has sought so passionately the audience cannot fail to be repelled by her promiscuity.

In the tragedies the amount of kissing and by-play which may be inferred from the text is sufficient to arouse doubt as to the correctness of Mr Granville-Barker's opinion on this aspect of Shakespearian drama. When Richard II is parted from his Queen he kisses her thrice, first to 'unkiss the oath,' and then in a tender passage:

> One kiss shall stop our mouths, and dumbly part
> Thus give I mine, and thus take I thy heart.
> *Queen.* Give me mine own again;

from which it is evident that there is a long embrace, a parting, and then a further and, for reasons of theatrical expediency, a more passionate kiss. The scene is a pathetic one, and could not be played with other than a naturalistic technique.

Mr Granville-Barker, in the essay which has already been quoted, says: 'For all the theme's passion, there is next to no physical love-making in *Romeo and Juliet.*' But there are three kisses in the play, the first when the lovers meet at the ball, which may well be two, the second when the lovers part for the last time, and the third which Paris gives Juliet in Friar Laurence's cell. It may be argued that three is no great number, but the point is that Shakespeare does not exclude physical love - making from his plays entirely, and it is more probable that good taste prevented him from exhibiting scenes of passion without nobility, rather than any fear for the capabilities of his boy actors.

Not only does Shakespeare introduce frequent kisses into his plays, but he employs variations on this theme to provide striking dramatic effects, such as that in *Romeo and Juliet* where the hero, thinking his wife to be dead, kisses her before he drinks the poison. The scene is a deeply moving one and the lines:

> Eyes, look your last!
> Arms, take your last embrace! and, lips, O you,
> The doors of breath, seal with a righteous kiss
> A dateless bargain to engrossing death!

come almost at its climax, when the dramatist would not risk any piece of business which might distract his audience or cause it to be amused. A similar effect is used in *Othello* when Desdemona is murdered. Her husband kisses her as she sleeps, and when he himself is at the point of death, he drags himself to her bed 'to die upon a kiss.' In both these instances the kiss is used to bring about a deeply pathetic effect, and it is significant that the whole of the acting burden falls upon the adult actor, but it is the boy who plays Desdemona or Juliet who is kissed, and if there had been anything ridiculous or embarrassing in such an action either to the boy or to the audience, these scenes would certainly have been written differently.

It is difficult to know quite what Mr Granville-Barker means by 'cruder phases of the emotional traffic between male and female.' There are not only kisses enough in Shakespeare, but there are several

scenes which could hardly be performed without
caresses of some sort, probably not very unlike those
used on the modern stage, for any phase of emotional
traffic which is too crude destroys dramatic illusion
by its personal message to the audience, and yet an
attempt on the stage to minimize or scamp scenes of
love-making is certain to be noticed with amusement
by the spectators. Actors and dramatists have to
steer a wise middle course between scenes of too great
realism and those where realism is obviously avoided,
when romantic love is to be shown on the stage. It
would be difficult to present the last Act of *The Merchant
of Venice*, however, without some indication that
Lorenzo and Jessica are deeply in love; the poetry
about the beauty of the night is probably meant as an
indication of that heightened appreciation of nature
which is supposed to be a prerogative of lovers, and
the 'out-nighting' would seem very flat unless the love
which inspires it were indicated by an embrace of some
sort. A scene which demands a show of physical
passion is that in *Titus Andronicus* in which Tamora
attempts to cheer Aaron with her embraces. The discussion of the play in Chapter III treats of this aspect
of the scene, but it is necessary to introduce it again
here in order to make clear the part which physical
love-making has in the technique of Shakespeare's
plays. It is very probable that the embraces of these
two, or Tamora's blandishments, would be represented as larger than life, which by no means decreases
the difficulties they provide for the actor. Tamora
is a stock character of all drama, the Amazon or

Unprincipled Woman, and no audience would be content unless she gave some demonstration of her power to subjugate men by her physical charms.

This discussion of the extent to which the cruder phases of emotional traffic between men and women are represented in Shakespeare would not be complete without a further reference to the scene between Falstaff and Doll Tearsheet in the tavern at Eastcheap, to which the words 'crude' and 'traffic' may fittingly be applied. The scene is, of course, one of raffish comedy, and although the references in the text from which specific gestures and embraces may be deduced are not many, they are sufficient to dispose of any notion that an actor subject to embarrassment could ever play the part. The by-play which prompts the Prince's:

> Look whether the wither'd elder hath not his poll claw'd like a parrot,

and Poins's rejoinder:

> Is it not strange that desire should so many years outlive performance?

is of no merely formal kind, and it is followed by Falstaff's:

> Thou dost give me flattering busses.

At this point the reader may be reminded of Herrick's epigram:

> Kissing and bussing, differ both in this,
> We busse our Wantons, but our Wives we kisse.
> (*Hesperides*, 513.)

On the Elizabethan stage this scene would no doubt be

played most realistically, and if the boy or youth who
undertook Doll were not good in his part the spectators would show their disapproval very rapidly. It
has already been suggested that the part was played
by a boy of more than the usual age, as he would be
more likely to appreciate both the humorous and the
mordant aspects of the character.

These remarks do not pretend to include all the
instances where Shakespeare uses embraces or kisses
in his plays to represent romantic or filial love, but a
sufficient number of examples has been presented to
make it clear that there was no prejudice against such
devices, and their use in tragedy shows that the
audience was not likely to regard them as funny. It
may also be assumed that as so many embraces occur
in the plays the sort of by-play which might lead up
to them was also employed, and that such a character
as Cressida might be well supplied with flirtatious
looks and gestures. There is reference to the:

. . . strange oeillades and most speaking looks,

which Goneril directed against Edmund, and the 'leer
of invitation' which Falstaff wrongfully ascribed to
Mrs Ford may well have had its place in the equipment
of the boy actor. There can be very little doubt that
the boys were skilled in the means of presenting love,
whether romantic or comic, upon the stage, and it is
unlikely that it cost them anything in embarrassment
to do so. It seems needless to attribute to the boy
actor a squeamishness in this regard which training
as an actor very soon removes in anybody. The

o

Elizabethan theatre was the home of a wonderful variety of conventions, but in this matter the audiences seem to have demanded and received a considerable amount of realism. For the laſt time in this book let the angry Prynne speak on the matter:

> Survey we but a whiles, *those venomous unchaſte, inceſtuous kisses* (as the *Fathers* ſtile them:) those wanton dalliances, those meretricious imbracements, complements; those enchanting, powerfull, overcomming sollicitations unto lewdnesse; *those immodeſt geſtures*, speeches, attires, which inseparably accompany the aċting of our Stage-playes; especially where the Bawdes, the Panders, the Lovers, the Wooers, the Adulterers, the Womans or Love-sicke persons parts are lively represented, (whose poysonous filthinesse I dare not fully anatomize, for feare it should infeċt, not mend the Reader,) muſt needs at firſt acknowledge, the very aċtion of our Stage-Playes to be execrably obscene.

What the audience thought about the effeċt of such behaviour on the boys it is impossible to tell but it may be guessed that they were, for one reason or another, indifferent to the matter. They may well have been unconscious that the eſteem in which the boys were held and the parts which they were called upon to play could have had any pernicious effeċt either upon the boys or upon themselves; to be indifferent to an evil is often to disarm it.

Although the boy aċtors were important in the Elizabethan theatre there is no evidence to suggeſt that they were in any respeċt eſteemed as the equals of the adult aċtors within the company itself, and there is a considerable body of reasonable conjeċture to show that they were not, and that they worked under that sort of discipline which exiſts where the maſters of a craft and apprentices to it are engaged in a common effort.

There has been no attempt in this work to assign parts in Shakespeare's plays to those members of his company whose names are known, except for one supposition in the case of Robert Goffe, to which no importance is attached. An elaborate system of hazard and conjecture has led T. W. Baldwin, in *The Organization and Personnel of the Shakespearean Company* (1927), to determine the actors of most of the parts, and readers who are interested will wish to consult his book. As the information surviving about these actors is scanty in the extreme, however, the mere attaching of their names to certain roles is a fruitless task.

This discussion of the influence of the boy actor upon Shakespeare's dramatic technique is now almost complete, for it remains only to integrate the conclusions reached in individual passages and to attempt to determine the extent to which the boy actor convention should govern the conduct of the modern actress in a Shakespearian role.

It cannot successfully be maintained that the convention of the boy actor placed any crippling restraint upon Shakespeare's invention, nor is any one likely to hold, with Lord Chesterfield, that his female characterization is coarse and inadequate. It is clear that the performances of the boy actors were satisfactory to the audiences and to the playwrights who have left passages complimentary to them in their works.

An examination of the plays with intent to consider

the various roles in them from the point of view of the actor reveals that the women's parts are noticeably easier to act than those of the men, and that this is the result of a number of technical devices which contrive to shift the burden of the heavy acting from the woman to the man in scenes where they appear to be in conflict. It is not suggested that this was in every case the conscious and laborious intention of the author, but only that it was a part of his technique of writing to adjust his female roles to the resources of the boys who filled them. In comedy, where the chief requirements of the actor are technical skill and personal charm, the women's roles are of first importance, for these were the qualities which the boy actors might be expected to have in a high degree. In the histories women play little part, and their roles are written chiefly to supply tender relief from the stress of the scenes of intrigue and battle. It is significant that in the histories, where the general level of acting must have been strenuous, the chief female roles are those of old women, parts which were played by men who could vie successfully with the adult actors in their power of delivery and their ability to wrest the attention of the audience to themselves.

The women of the tragedies are, on the whole, less important than those of the comedies, and in the great tragedies of *Hamlet*, *Lear*, *Macbeth*, and *Othello* they are markedly inferior to the men. It is only in the cases of Cleopatra and Juliet that a woman is a tragic protagonist, and in these plays the quality of tragedy is less intense than in the others, principally on this account. It is no accident that, in the four tragedies mentioned above, the heroes are all shown labouring under a mental burden which makes a radical change in their characters, and that the heroines are static figures in whom no change is apparent except a violent change from sanity to madness in the cases of Ophelia and Lady Macbeth. Because of the limitations of his boy actors, Shakespeare never presents a woman who is engaged in a violent mental struggle.

It seems clear that Shakespeare wanted his tragic heroes to stand alone in their splendour and that the modern method of producing the plays in which the tragic heroines are bolstered up with a false importance results in a distortion of his original conception. This distortion is particularly evident in *Macbeth*, where Lady Macbeth now rivals her husband as the most important figure in the play and very frequently acts him off the stage because she has not sufficient artistic conscience to keep in her proper place in the scheme of the action. Very few actors have the power to overcome the efforts of a really selfish actress who determines to shine at his expense, and at the expense of the play, in a part in which only a fool could fail. Unhappily too many actresses are without bowels in artistic matters, and, as these take an essentially low view of their art, it becomes in their hands mere self-exploitation. Feminine intuition and the extravagances of fretted nerves are not adequate substitutes for technique and classical chastity and economy in acting. Perhaps it may be said that Shakespeare spoke by means of the boy actor, whereas the modern audience must often feel that he speaks in spite of the actress.

The author would be most unhappy if this work were taken to reflect unfavourably upon the actresses who have graced the stage since Mrs Hughes's appearance in 1660, or to hold in contempt an art which he worships (this side idolatry) as much as any. It is undeniable that actresses are able to sustain much more vigorous roles than any Shakespeare wrote for his boys; it would be ridiculous to quarrel with a change in stage convention which has given to the world Mrs Alving and Hedda Gabler, parts beyond the skill and comprehension of the most gifted boy. Still, it is unwise when studying a Shakespearian heroine to dismiss the boy actor without a careful consideration of his capabilities and the part which these played in the formation of Shakespeare's dramatic technique. The great artist turns to account the very limitations of his medium, and this is what Shakespeare has done in the creation of the most remarkable company of women in English drama.

The actress who attempts to reconstruct a Shakespearian heroine in terms of the boy actor will meet with several difficulties. First of all, she must dismiss from her mind any notions of child actors which she may have gleaned from the infant prodigies of the cinema. The skill of these remarkably clever children lies in exploiting their own natural charm *as* children, and in causing the springs of doting parental affection to gush in the hearts of their admirers. Nor may she learn anything useful from the accounts written of

*Master Betty, the young Roscius, born at Shrewsbury,
13th September* 1791

GABRIELLE ENTHOVEN COLLECTION, VICTORIA
AND ALBERT MUSEUM

performances by such oddities as Master William Henry West Betty (1791–1874), called 'The Young Roscius,' whose performances, though remarkable, were largely copied from the best adult actors of his day. The actress who embarks on such a feat of reconstruction will only be able to do so by considering the circumstances of the Elizabethan theatre, and the training and capabilities of the boy actors who played in it.

If any actress wonders why she should put herself to this bother let her be assured that it will save her much trouble and vexation in the long run, provided, of course, that she cares at all for her art and wants to do her best in the role given to her. If she considers her part from the point of view of the boy actor, it will emerge as a simple and direct conception, which she can bring to life with clarity and purpose; she will be spared the necessity to deal with complexities which are not inherent in the part but which result from a wrong notion of it, and she will find her part a vehicle for what is best in herself as an artist, and not merely for mannerism and self-display. When she has a clear notion of her role from the boy actor's point of view she may inject into it just as much of herself and of her particular feminine quality as her artistic conscience will allow, and the result should be a performance with a clear and coherent outline, shorn of irrelevant and irritating externals and presenting the part in the brilliant colours in which Shakespeare drew it.

It is only by achieving this simplicity that the artist can hope to become a worthy interpreter of

Shakespeare's female roles.   The actress who abandons
the policy of consciously exploiting her own charm
will gain the universal quality which must have been
the great attraction of the best of the boy actors.   Mr
Bernard Shaw has said, in one of his dramatic
criticisms (*Our Theatre in the Nineties*, vol. i):

> Woman's great art is to lie low and let the imagination of
> the male endow her with depths,

and this was also true of the boy actors who presented
the outward seeming of feminine beauty, grace, and
distinction of speech; their audiences were not slow
to project upon them the qualities which they most
valued in women, and thus endowed the parts they
played with the charm of the ideal, rather than the real.

From time to time, in the pages of modern criticism,
there are references to the boy actors which show an
increasing realization of their value as interpretive
artists.   The following passage from Sir Walter
Raleigh's study, *Shakespeare* (1901), brought down a
storm of protest when first it appeared, and because of
its truth it is quoted here:

> In spite of all this it may be doubted whether Shakespeare
> has not suffered more than he has gained by the genius of
> latter-day actresses, who bring into the plays a realism and
> robust emotion which sometimes obscure the sheer poetic
> value of the author's conception.   The boys were no doubt
> very highly trained and amenable to instruction; so that the
> parts of Rosalind and Desdemona may well have been
> rendered with a clarity and simplicity which served as a
> transparent medium for the author's wit and pathos.
> Poetry, like religion, is outraged when it is made a platform
> for the exhibition of their own talent and passion by those
> who are its ministers.   With the disappearance of the boy

players the poetic drama died in England, and it has had no second life.

The revival of the convention of the boy actors is neither advisable nor practicable. It remains, therefore, for the actresses of to-day and to-morrow to study to give us what was best in the boy actors' as well as what is best in their own art. And by this means, though the poetic drama may not revive again in England, the drama of Shakespeare may live anew.

NOTES

THE line references in the following notes correspond to the *New Temple* edition of Shakespeare's plays, for convenience in reference. The quotations in the text, however, sometimes employ variant readings where these have been considered preferable.

NOTES TO CHAPTER II

1. *Hamlet*, Act III, Scene II, lines 40–7.
2. *The Comedy of Errors*, Act II, Scene I.
3. *Ibid.* Act III, Scene II.
4. *Ibid.* Act IV, Scene II, lines 25–8.
5. *The Taming of the Shrew*, Act I, Scene I, line 55.
6. *Ibid.* Act I, Scene I, lines 70–1.
7. *Ibid.* Act I, Scene I, lines 92–101.
8. *Ibid.* Act I, Scene I, lines 105–44.
9. *Ibid.* Act I, Scene II.
10. *Ibid.* Act II, Scene I.
11. *Ibid.* Act II, Scene I, lines 142–59.
12. *Ibid.* Act III, Scene II.
13. *The Two Gentlemen of Verona*, Act I, Scene II.
14. *As You Like It*, Act I, Scene II.
15. *Twelfth Night*, Act I, Scene II.
16. *The Two Gentlemen of Verona*, Act I, Scene II.
17. *Ibid.* Act IV, Scene IV, lines 91–108 and 180–206.
18. *Love's Labour's Lost*, Act II, Scene I, lines 13–14.
19. *Ibid.* Act IV, Scene I.
20. *A Midsummer Night's Dream*, Act I, Scene I, lines 180–251.
21. *Ibid.* Act II, Scene II, lines 35–65.
22. *Ibid.* Act I, Scene II, lines 145–56.
23. *Ibid.* Act I, Scene I, lines 226–51.
24. *The Merchant of Venice*, Act I, Scene I, lines 161–76.
25. *Ibid.* Act II, Scene I.

26. *The Merchant of Venice*, Act III, Scene II.
27. *Ibid.* Act II, Scene IV, lines 33–8.
28. *Ibid.* Act III, Scene IV, lines 62–79.
29. *Much Ado About Nothing*, Act IV, Scene I, lines 254–331.
30. *Ibid.* Act III, Scene I, lines 107–16.
31. *Ibid.* Act II, Scene III, lines 207–32 and 242–49.
32. *Ibid.* Act III, Scene IV.
33. *As You Like It*, Act I, Scene II.
34. *Ibid.* Act I, Scene II, lines 240–1.
35. *Ibid.* Act IV, Scene I.
36. *Twelfth Night*, Act I, Scene IV, lines 30–4.
37. *Ibid.* Act I, Scene V, lines 167–235.
38. *Ibid.* Act II, Scene II, lines 16–40.
39. *Ibid.* Act II, Scene IV.
40. *Ibid.* Act IV, Scene III.
41. *The Merry Wives of Windsor*, Act III, Scene III, lines 19–22.
42. *Ibid.* Act V, Scene V.
43. *All's Well that Ends Well*, Act I, Scene I, lines 76–95.
44. *Ibid.* Act I, Scene I, lines 213–26.
45. *Measure for Measure*, Act I, Scene II.
46. *Henry IV, Part II*, Act V, Scene IV.
47. *Measure for Measure*, Act II, Scene II, lines 162–88; and Scene IV, lines 1–30.
48. *Ibid.* Act III, Scene I.
49. *Ibid.* Act III, Scene I, lines 136–51.
50. *Ibid.* Act II, Scene IV, line 185.
51. This is the arrangement of the editors of the New Cambridge Edition.
52. *The Comedy of Errors*, Act III, Scene III.
53. *Ibid.* Act IV, Scene I, lines 110–11; Act IV, Scene IV, line 153; and Act V, lines 413–15.
54. *Love's Labour's Lost*, Act I, Scene II, lines 122–39.
55. *Ibid.* Act IV, Scene I, lines 60–88.

NOTES TO CHAPTER III

1. *Henry VI, Part I*, Act V, Scene IV.
2. *Henry VI, Part II*, Act I, Scene I.

3. *Henry VI, Part II*, Act I, Scene III.

4. *Ibid.* Act III, Scene II, lines 73–121.

5. *Ibid.* Act III, Scene II, line 343.

6. *Ibid.* Act IV, Scene IV.

7. *Henry VI, Part III*, Act II, Scene II, line 176.

8. *Ibid.* Act V, Scene V, line 29.

9. *Ibid.* Act I, Scene IV, lines 111–49 and 152–68.

10. *Ibid.* Act I, Scene IV, line 114.

11. *Ibid.* Act III, Scene II.

12. *Richard III*, Act I, Scene II.

13. *Ibid.* Act I, Scene II, lines 152–84.

14. *Ibid.* Act I, Scene II, lines 193–203.

15. *Ibid.* Act I, Scene II, lines 228–64.   Lady Anne also refers to it in Act IV, Scene I, lines 80–83.

16. *Ibid.* Act IV, Scene I, lines 100–6.

17. *Ibid.* Act IV, Scene IV.

18. *Richard II*, Act II, Scene II; and Act III, Scene IV.

19. *Ibid.* Act III, Scene I.

20. *Henry IV, Part II*, Act II, Scene III.

21. *Henry IV, Part I*, Act II, Scene III.

22. *Henry VIII*, Act I, Scene IV.

23. *Titus Andronicus*, Act I, Scene I, line 52.

24. *Ibid.* Act II, Scene I.

25. *Ibid.* Act II, Scene II, lines 16–17

26. *Ibid.* Act II, Scene III, lines 66–71.

27. *Ibid.* Act II, Scene III, lines 147, 172, 174, and 182.

28. *Ibid.* Act II, Scene IV.

29. *Ibid.* Act II, Scene IV.

30. *Ibid.* Act IV, Scene I.

31. *Ibid.* Act II, Scene IV.

32. *Ibid.* Act III, Scene I.

33. *Ibid.* Act II, Scene IV.

34. *Ibid.* Act II, Scene IV.

35. *Ibid.* Act I, Scene I.

36. *Ibid.* Act II, Scene III.

37. *Ibid.* Act II, Scene III.

38. *Ibid.* Act II, Scene III, lines 51–2.

39. *Ibid.* Act II, Scene III, lines 188–91.

40. *Ibid.* Act V, Scene II.

41. *Julius Caesar*, Act II, Scene i.
42. *Ibid.* Act I, Scene ii.
43. *Ibid.* Act I, Scene ii, lines 6–9.
44. *Ibid.* Act II, Scene ii.
45. *Pericles*, Act I, Scene ii.
46. *Ibid.* Act IV, Scene i.
47. *Ibid.* Act IV, Scene ii.
48. *Ibid.* Act IV, Scene iv.
49. *Measure for Measure*, Act II, Scene ii.
50. *Pericles*, Act IV, Scene vi, lines 156–64 and 169–82.
51. *Troilus and Cressida*, Act I, Scene i, lines 47–62.
52. *Ibid.* Act I, Scene ii.
53. *Ibid.* Act I, Scene ii, lines 280–93.
54. *Ibid.* Act III, Scene ii.
55. *Ibid.* Act III, Scene ii, lines 113–29.
56. *Ibid.* Act III, Scene ii, lines 166–79 and 179–91.
57. *Ibid.* Act IV, Scene ii, lines 37–9.
58. *Ibid.* Act IV, Scene iv.
59. *Ibid.* Act III, Scene ii, line 49.
60. *Ibid.* Act III, Scene ii, line 57.
61. *Ibid.* Act III, Scene ii, lines 129–34.
62. *Ibid.* Act IV, Scene v.
63. *Ibid.* Act IV, Scene v, lines 54–63.
64. *Ibid.* Act V, Scene i, lines 97–8.
65. *Ibid.* Act V, Scene ii, lines 104–9.
66. *Ibid.* Act II, Scene ii, line 100.
67. *Cymbeline*, Act I, Scene i, lines 130–1.
68. *Ibid.* Act I, Scene vi, lines 112–13.
69. *Ibid.* Act III, Scene iv, lines 100–2.
70. *Ibid.* Act III, Scene vi.
71. *Ibid.* Act IV, Scene ii, lines 292–333.
72. *Ibid.* Act I, Scene vi.
73. *Romeo and Juliet*, Act II, Scene iii.
74. *Ibid.* Act III, Scene i, lines 109–15.
75. *Ibid.* Act III, Scene v, lines 62–6.
76. *Ibid.* Act III, Scene v, lines 71–128.
77. *Ibid.* Act IV, Scene i, lines 77–88.
78. *Ibid.* Act V, Scene i.
79. *Hamlet*, Act III, Scene iv.

80. *Hamlet*, Act IV, Scene VII, lines 167–84.
81. *Ibid.* Act V, Scene I, lines 244–7.
82. *Ibid.* Act I, Scene III.
83. *Ibid.* Act I, Scene III, lines 45–51.
84. *Ibid.* Act III, Scene I, lines 152–63.
85. *Ibid.* Act III, Scene II, lines 113–25.
86. *Ibid.* Act IV, Scene V.
87. *Othello*, Act V, Scene II, lines 112–74.
88. *Ibid.* Act III, Scene III.
89. *Ibid.* Act II, Scene III, lines 326–78.
90. *Ibid.* Act IV, Scene II, lines 112–73.
91. *King Lear*, Act I, Scene I, lines 124–5.
92. *Ibid.* Act I, Scene I, lines 285–308.
93. *Ibid.* Act II, Scene IV, line 155.
94. *Ibid.* Act II, Scene IV, lines 263–84.
95. *Ibid.* Act V, Scene III.
96. *Macbeth*, Act I, Scene V.
97. *Ibid.* Act II, Scene III.
98. *Ibid.* Act III, Scene II.
99. *Antony and Cleopatra*, Act II, Scene V, lines 18–23.
100. *Ibid.* Act II, Scene II, lines 190–245.
101. *Ibid.* Act II, Scene V.
102. *Ibid.* Act IV, Scene XV.
103. *Ibid.* Act IV, Scene XV, lines 59–68 and 72–90.
104. *Ibid.* Act V, Scene II, lines 216–21.

NOTES TO CHAPTER IV

1. *Henry V*, Act III, Scene IV.
2. *Henry VIII*, Act II, Scene III.
3. *Richard II*, Act V, Scene II.
4. *Henry VI, Part II*, Act I, Scene III.
5. *Ibid.* Act II, Scene III.
6. *Richard III.*   As in Act II, Scene II, lines 66–88.
7. *Ibid.* Act II, Scene IV.
8. *Ibid.* Act IV, Scene IV, lines 85–118.
9. *King John*, Act I, Scene I.
10. *Ibid.* Act III, Scenes I and IV.
11. *Pericles*, Act IV, Scene I.

12. *Cymbeline*, Act III, Scene i, lines 14–33.
13. *The Winter's Tale*, Act II, Scene iii.
14. *Ibid.* Act III, Scene ii.
15. *All's Well that Ends Well*, Act I, Scene i, lines 57–68.
16. *Ibid.* Act I, Scene iii.
17. *Coriolanus*, Act II, Scene i, lines 179–80.
18. *Ibid.* Act III, Scene ii.
19. *Ibid.* Act IV, Scene i.
20. *Ibid.* Act V, Scene iii, lines 94–125 and 131–82.
21. *Henry VIII*, Act I, Scene ii.
22. *Ibid.* Act II, Scene iv.
23. *Ibid.* Act III, Scene i.
24. *Ibid.* Act IV, Scene ii.
25. *Measure for Measure*, Act I, Scene ii.
26. *Henry IV, Part I*, Act II, Scene iv.
27. *Ibid.* Act III, Scene iii.
28. *Henry V*, Act II, Scene iii.
29. *Henry IV, Part II*, Act II, Scene iv.
30. *Romeo and Juliet*, Act I, Scene iii.
31. *Ibid.* Act II, Scene v.
32. *Ibid.* Act II, Scene iv.
33. *Richard III*, Act II, Scene ii.
34. *The Merry Wives of Windsor*, Act IV, Scene i.
35. *The Winter's Tale*, Act II, Scene i.
36. *Ibid.* Act I, Scene i.
37. *Henry V*, Act III, Scene ii, lines 29–56.
38. *Ibid.* Act IV, Scene iv.
39. *Ibid.* Act IV, Scene vii.
40. *King John*, Act II, Scene i, lines 12–17.
41. *Ibid.* Act IV, Scene i.
42. *A Midsummer Night's Dream*, Act II, Scene i, lines
    81–117.

BIBLIOGRAPHY

THE works chiefly used in the preparation of this study are listed here. Others which were used incidentally are referred to in the text.

BALDWIN, I. W., *The Organization and Personnel of the Shakespearean Company*, 1927.

Cambridge History of English Literature, The, vols. v and vi, 1934.

CHAMBERS, SIR E. K., *William Shakespeare*, 1930.

CHAMBERS, SIR E. K., *The Medieval Stage* (2 vols.), 1913.

CHAMBERS, SIR E. K., *The Elizabethan Stage* (4 vols.), 1923.

CHAPMAN, GEORGE, *Plays* (ed. Parrott).

CIBBER, COLLEY, *Apology for the Life of Mr Colley Cibber, Comedian*, 1740.

DOWNES, JOHN, *Roscius Anglicanus*, 1708.

GRANVILLE-BARKER, H., *Prefaces to Shakespeare*: Series I, 1927; Series II, 1930; Series III, 1934.

GRANVILLE-BARKER, H., and HARRISON, G. B. (editors), *A Companion to Shakespeare Studies*, 1934.

GREG, W. W., *Henslowe's Diary* (2 vols.), 1904.

HARRISON, G. B., *Shakespeare at Work*, 1933.

HAZLITT, W. C. (editor), *Shakespeare's Library* (6 vols.) (2nd edition), 1875.

JONSON, BEN, *Plays* (ed. Gifford).

LAWRENCE, W. J., *The Physical Conditions of the Elizabethan Public Playhouse*, 1927.

MASEFIELD, JOHN, *Shakespeare*, 1911.

NICOLL, ALLARDYCE, *British Drama* (3rd edition), 1932.

POEL, WILLIAM, *Shakespeare in the Theatre*, 1913

RIDLEY, M. R., *Shakespeare's Plays : A Commentary*, 1937.

MADE AT THE
TEMPLE PRESS LETCHWORTH
IN GREAT BRITAIN